Please Don't Shoot!
I'm Already Wounded.

Maria Anne Hirschmann

PLEASE DON'T SHOOT!

I'm Already Wounded.

The Story of a Heartbreak and a Ministry

Tyndale House
Publishers, Inc.
Wheaton, Illinois

Quotations from *The
Spiritual Man* by Watchman
Nee are used by permission
of Christian Fellowship
Publishers, Inc., New York.

Library of Congress
Catalog Card Number
78-58744

ISBN 0-8423-4837-9,
paper

Second printing,
March 1979.

Printed in the United States
of America.

This is a true story. Some names, places, and times have been changed to avoid embarrassment.

The story has been written with the lifeblood of a wounded heart—mine. God showed me that it is now time to write it—so that other wounded hearts might find new hope and joy in HIM.

Hansi-Maria

AUGUST/ *Sunday Morning*

Morning dawn—my cherished hour of the day. I sit in my favorite place above our mountain home and look toward the horizon, waiting for the first ray of light. I wonder if it will come. It might stay gray, cloudy, smoggy, miserable.

It seems as though life has left the mountain. The ground is dusty, the grass dry and brown, the rocks dark and naked against the sky. Sultry smoke-filled air hangs heavy above me and covers the valley below. I wonder if the forest fire is under control by now. It's behind our mountain and a long way off yet, but the smoke and the ashes have penetrated everything and darkened the sun for days.

My heart feels as heavy as the air. I am almost too numb to think, too confused to pray. I cannot understand why I can't even talk to God. For the last three years I have done it so often right here on this spot. Ever since we moved up here, this has been my special place for prayer, meditation, and collecting my thoughts.

I had such high hopes and everybody in the family seemed so excited and positive when we first leased the place. Everybody? Well, at least the children and I had bubbled with joy. Looking back now I begin to wonder if

my husband was ever happy about it. He never said anything to discourage the move. I knew it was not very practical when we did it. It meant that I had to get up at the
crack of dawn, get three children ready for school, and
leave before seven o'clock in the morning. Then I had
to drive forty-nine miles one way to go teach in the city.

To me it was worth it. I am a mountain girl, and I
never liked living in a city or large town. We had lived
cramped and hemmed in by houses and neighbors ever
since Rollie and I got married more than twenty-five years
ago. Well, it wasn't the only thing that cramped our
life-style from the beginning. Poverty edged too close for
comfort, and so did many other problems. Come to think
of it, life has been one big long struggle for me, as long as
I can remember.

My childhood began on the wrong side of the tracks.
Before my mama died she gave me, a small baby, to a
peasant family. They lived in a simple cottage in a small
mountain village which was surrounded by deep
evergreen woods. I grew up with hunger, loneliness, and
rejection because my foster family was very poor and no
one wanted or needed me very badly. I was kept there
for pity's and God's sake. It was in my lonely childhood
that I learned to love the trees and mountains so very
much. Or maybe I loved them because of the loneliness.
Evergreen trees became my friends long before people
did. My few happy childhood memories are of a hayloft
where I slept and the mountain woods where I roamed,
searching for mushrooms, firewood, and wild berries. I
never lost my *Heimweh* (nostalgia) for the mountains,
ever.

When I left my mountain village in Czechoslovakia at
the age of fourteen, I somehow knew I would never
return to it. I didn't.

Life took me through rough waters and brought me
halfway around the globe. But wherever I lived, I longed
and searched for the sound I loved the most: the song of
the mountain wind in a fir tree.

When we moved to our cabin three years ago, I
thought that I had come home at last. My heart sang and
everybody smiled a lot at first. I put my bed on the
screened-in porch so that I could see the stars and wait
for the night wind to rustle in the big black oak trees. I
wasn't even disappointed that the desert mountains had
no spruce or fir trees. Every so often I would slip out
quietly and climb to my prayer spot. God never seemed
nearer than when I lifted my heart and hands to him in
the deep silence of a beginning or dying day on the top
of my new mountain.

Strangely enough, I never realized how lonely I was
until we moved here. My need drove me more and more
often to my prayer place and very close to God.

I had such high hopes that we would grow closer
together as a family in our secluded place, but it seemed
to work out just the opposite way. My husband, Rollie,
had never spent much time at home before, and now he
was around even less. Timothy, our older son, found the
wrong crowd again. He was one of the reasons I had
pushed so hard to get out of the city. I hoped that if we
got him away from the influence of his pot-smoking
friends, he would once again become sweet and
easygoing. I dreamed of cozy family evenings at the
fireplace with Bible stories and long discussions. I
dreamed wrong. Sure, the fireplace crackled through the
cool seasons with its warm fires, but the family
togetherness never happened.

The television was one of the worst intrusions. One of
Rollie's doctor friends had given us that one-eyed, color
monster as a Christmas gift. I pleaded. I reasoned. I
argued. Many promises were given; strict rules were
laid—and broken, mainly by Rollie. I would forbid the
kids to watch those horrible shows of violence and
bloodshed. Rollie would come home and turn them on.
The children would quickly work their way into the living
room and watch with dad while I would work or sit alone
in the kitchen. When I made myself watch it, in order to

be with the family, I'd end up physically ill and go without sleep for nights. I had seen too much *real* pain and agony to tolerate their enactment on programs.

The wrong TV shows were not the only thing to keep me from peaceful nights. My worries about Tim were harder to conquer. I envied Rollie. He managed to sleep in sorrow or joy. Sleep seemed to be his escape from any disturbance or problem. He would snore in the room next to the porch, regardless of what happened. Wide awake, I would stare into the night, praying and crying softly into my pillows.

It went from bad to worse when Timothy moved out. We had a big confrontation and I felt terrible. I wasn't sorry for what I had said, but for how I said it. I explained to my son what God had shown me after much prayer, but I lost my cool when I said it and we ended up yelling at each other. That night I crawled into my bed and had just one wish—I wanted to die!

Rollie seldom got involved in our family happenings. He was too preoccupied with his studies and personal cares. I was mom to him as much and more than to the children. I always tried to shield him from too many upheavals. He would get so upset that he brought on more problems. Rollie would either say nothing or he would lose his temper so badly that the tension and pain were only increased.

He had nothing to say when Tim moved out. Our older son moved to the village below the mountain—into a house full of young dropouts who made their living in various—but mostly illegal—ways.

Rollie and I had so little to say to each other that it should have alarmed me. But we were all so busy and caught up in living, it never dawned on me that our home could ever break up. Such things happened to other people, not to us. *It couldn't happen to us, it just couldn't!*

But it did! And the straw that broke the camel's back

was my ulcer. I asked Rollie to leave for a while. He
packed his suitcase last week and drove away. He called
me later and gave me the address of his apartment and
his telephone number. Now the cabin is empty. Timothy
still lives in the village. Kathy and Heidi are working in a
summer camp. Peter is a camper at the same place. And
Tina and her husband are still overseas with the army. I
was left behind to dissolve the home. It was hard,
emotionally and physically. I didn't want anyone to know
about it, so I worked all by myself. I got my back
completely out of shape dragging mattresses down the
narrow stairs. The moving of the furniture wasn't so bad.
I could dismantle it into bearable sizes to carry it out.

Now it is done. I am waiting for the truck to move it.
When my friends find out that I didn't ask for any help
with the moving, I'll get into trouble. By then I hope to
be able to explain it to them. Right now I can't. I cannot
talk about it at all. Not to anybody, not even to God. I
am sitting here at my prayer spot and I have no words
left in me. I know this is another last time. I'll never come
back to this specific place again. It's another end in my
life. I am numb, hurt, raw inside from unshed tears. I
don't dare to cry. I might crack up. My heart is beginning
to form one single sentence. The words are repeating
themselves in my mind like a needle which is stuck on a
phonograph record. Though my lips cannot move, my
heart is begging: "Help me, God, please help me. Don't
leave me, God, don't leave me. I am so alone. . . ."

SEPTEMBER/ *Saturday Morning*

I am lying on the carpet in front of the fake fireplace in
my new city apartment. I just came back from church. I
didn't stay long. I walked in and it just so happened that I
turned around unexpectedly. I saw two "saints" stick their
heads together and whisper. It was very obvious that they

talked about me. They both looked in my direction and when I turned around and looked at them, they quit talking and sat very straight. Their eyes kept on speaking, though, with cold disapproval and righteous indignation.

I got up and walked out and hundreds of eyes seemed to burn holes in my back when I left. Another final moment. I shall never enter this building again! I was hardly greeted when I entered. Nobody said good-bye or came after me as I departed. And the announcements of the home missionary leader droned in my ears as I walked to my car. He was in the middle of reporting on a new neighborhood program that was well on the way. He sounded very excited about it. Several church members had signed up a large number of people for a Bible correspondence course of the denomination. The numbers sounded impressive. Numbers seemed so important to that man. He repeated the total over and over. Numbers, numbers—everywhere. The numbers of the hymns on the announcement board. The number of people who attended last week. The amount of the offering as compared to the same date last year. The numbers had increased all the way. Good! They wouldn't miss me at all. I was only one number—a minus among the many pluses and successes of their missionary efforts.

I came back to my silent apartment and turned on the radio. My minister's sermon was broadcasted each week for the benefit of the shut-ins in the church community. I like the minister very much. He is young, well-educated, interesting, and apparently very sincere and eager to serve the Lord. Too bad he is so very busy with his big church; I think I could talk to him if he tried to see me. He never will; he doesn't even know I exist. I just moved back to the city and I am new in this particular church. However, many people know me.

Most people in my denomination know who I am. I have done a lot of writing and speaking for them in the last few years. It became one of the problems of my home that I was growing so popular among the churches. Rollie hated to be left behind whenever I was asked to speak or sing. In the beginning we did it together. Later the requests came in just for me. At first I refused to go alone. I didn't want to hurt Rollie's feelings. Whenever a call or letter came, I would ask God to show me what to do. He always said, "Go." I would argue with him that I had to consider my family's and husband's feelings first. Wasn't *that* the rule of the Book?

Luke 14:26 was the text that always rang in my mind like a bell. "If any man come to me, and hate not his father, and mother, and wife, and children, and brethren, and sisters, yea, and his own life also, he cannot be my disciple."

"What about my submission to my husband?" I asked God several times.

The same text, the same answer came every time.

I remember one early morning when I pleaded with God about the same issue up on my mountain spot.

"Go and talk to your husband and family about it," God said lovingly.

I brought it up at the breakfast table. It was the only time my whole family sat together, by my insistence. So far I had managed to enforce my rule that no radio or TV was to be turned on until we had had family worship after the morning meal. Since we ate so early it didn't interfere with the morning news, so Rollie didn't seem to mind.

"I have another invitation to speak next weekend. It is out of state," I said quietly. "I prayed about it and God seems to tell me that I must obey him and go. However, I do not feel that it is right for me to go against your will." I looked at Rollie. "After all, *you* are the head of the house, and if you forbid me to go, I am clear before God."

The children looked up and we all seemed to hold our breath. Everyone knew what a touchy subject I had brought up.

Rollie shifted uneasily. I knew that he hated to be put on the spot, but I seemed to have no choice. He looked down at his plate and shrugged his shoulders. "Do what you want. I know that God wants you to go, but I just don't want to be left alone. I shall *never* be alone. I don't like being alone. I hate it!"

"You are not alone when I am gone. The kids are here and would love to do some special things with you, Daddy." I wondered if I had kept the edge out of my voice. Another touchy subject! I seemed to nag him forever to spend more time with the kids. As a young teenager Peter needed him especially. I could see him going just the way Timothy went. And Timothy had gone through his teenage years without a father's attention. The fights and arguments we had about it were nothing to be proud of. I pleaded, cried, reasoned, fought—to no avail.

When Timothy moved out I got the blame. I took it. There was no doubt that it was my fault. After all, I was the only one who disciplined, ruled, and yelled. Timothy had a strict mother, and a father who was never home.

The morning discussion ended as usual. Rollie said, "Do what you want," and reached for the Bible in order to read something. Our devotional time had become a form—another family ritual, like brushing teeth and making the beds before leaving. I knew it, but I held on and insisted upon it although the family didn't care if we had it or not. I had been told that a family who prayed together stayed together, and I had believed it. I believed that daily devotions would keep a family together and I was wrong. I had believed so many things and formulas, and suddenly all I had trusted in on this earth had been shattered, and I didn't know anymore what to believe and what not to believe.

God was still real to me and so was his voice as I again prayed and listened to him. He was the only reality left in my life—he and my work. My life seemed to hang by a last tiny thread to that pivotal nail. The children were gone—by my decision. I had sent them to a private school in the Midwest. They had objected strongly. I didn't even discuss the matter. They went as soon as they returned from summer camp. I had no intention of drawing them day by day into the ugly conflict. I felt they were better off to live with it at a distance, at least for a little while.

Both girls left with many tears and perhaps much bitter feeling. Peter looked stunned. I tried to explain, but nobody heard me. Everybody was too broken up. Their world had shattered, too. They never dreamed that our home could break up. They watched their friends' parents getting divorces, but it had never dawned on them that it could happen in our home. They knew it couldn't happen because I had promised them that it would never happen to us.

The moment will be forever burned into my memory when Peter came back from school one day and said, "Mommy, Don's parents are getting a divorce." Don was Peter's best friend. Peter looked thoughtfully out the window for a long time and finally said, "Boy, am I glad that it could *never* happen in our family!"

I smiled and nodded. "You are right, Peter. It could *never* happen to this family. We stay together."

I meant it. I believed it. And then I broke my promise to Peter, and he is trying to figure out why his mother lied to him. He hasn't written me once since he left. The girls write very seldom and with an edge to their words.

"Lord, I always wondered how my neighbor survived when she lost her whole family in a car accident. I know now that death is not the most agonizing way to lose a whole family. Sweet memories and the assurance of reunion in heaven can soothe and heal the pain. But how does one cope with total loss *and* rejection, betrayal and utter confusion?"

The children are too perplexed to cope and I am no

help to them. I am groping for answers myself. We are all like islands that don't connect anymore.

If I did not have my classroom to go to, I think I would lose my mind. The students have no idea that I live alone. Most of the people at work don't know except for my principal and the office secretary. My students love me and I love them—more than ever before. I understand their confusion much better now. I teach high school dropouts and most of them come from broken or unhappy homes. I know now why they are so bewildered and lash out against adults and society. I begin to understand. . . .

OCTOBER/ *Friday Night*

Rollie called a few days ago and asked me to have dinner with him on our anniversary. We went to a Chinese restaurant and tried to talk. I ache for him, he looks so bad. He acted very self-confident and assured me that things were going well for him. But he has a hard time convincing me; I know him too well. We talked about the three younger kids—and money. I am carrying the entire financial load of their boarding school expenses, paying for insurance, clothing allowance, everything. My teacher's salary goes just so far and then I am at the end. We have no savings.

Rollie assured me that he had no money. I believed him. He always did have a hard time making ends meet. His childhood hadn't prepared him for a harsh life at all. He was the pampered only son of a well-to-do family. His grandmother, mother, and a servant girl had spoiled him up to the moment when he had to go to war as a young man. He quickly became an officer and had his own valet to jump at his commands. His family wired him money whenever his army pay wasn't enough. The end of World

War II brought the loss of his family's estate, refugee life in Western Germany, and our marriage.

He had never done any manual work before we married. He didn't know how! He tried, he really did. He was never very practical, but I loved his brilliant mind. He had fine talents, but not the kind that would bring financial stability. I always worked to help him pay our bills. I didn't mind, at least not the first twenty years of our togetherness. I hoped that someday Rollie would mature, get his degree, and take over. Yes, I hoped, waited, dreamed, coaxed, nagged, pushed . . . and tried to shield him whenever things got too rough for him. They did frequently—and God had shown me some painful things the night before our dinner date. I met Rollie at the restaurant. God had spoken very clearly to my heart, so clearly that I had no reason to question his orders.

"Take your hands off!" God said to me in the sleepless early hours of my morning. "Leave him alone. He must learn to lean on me, not on you. No man can live his life vicariously or believe in me through another person, not even his wife."

"What do I do if he wants to come back, Lord?" I asked. "Maybe his telephone call is an indication that he wants to start all over."

God's answer was very clear again. "Do not agree until I give you my permission."

"Lord," I said, "I am asked by more and more people why I am alone. What should I say?"

God answered, "Whatever your husband or others say about you, do not defend yourself at all. Trust me. I will defend you. Be still and wait. I shall lead you!" God had spoken and I knew it.

I told Rollie how God directed me. His face turned hard and his eyes looked like cold stones. "Are you accusing me of some terrible sin?"

"I accuse you of nothing, Rollie," I said very quietly.

"You don't need to worry that I will set a detective on your trail, or try to spy into your life. I don't have to. I am not responsible for you, only for myself. God will tell me what I have to do and when to do it. I can trust him. He will also provide for the children. He promised it."

We ate in silence. I finally looked up and said, "Rollie, you claim to be broke. Maybe you wouldn't be so bad off if you didn't spend so much money on telephone calls. You seem to have called every mutual friend we have across this nation, taking hours to tell them the most ugly, scandalous things about me." Rollie looked away.

"I tell nothing but the truth," he said. "You cannot prove a thing against me."

I tried again. "Rollie, do you realize what your gossip does to our children? You are telling half-truths and adding to the truth, leaving the rest to people's imagination."

"I can't help it if people's imaginations go wild," he said sullenly. "I never say anything you could sue me for."

"I am sure of that," I said, fighting back tears. "You word things so carefully that nobody could catch you even if he tried—and I am not trying to prove anything. I know I made many mistakes, but think of the damage you do to the young lives of our children when you call their mother terrible names. Do you truly believe what you say? You know better than that. We lived together for so long."

Rollie's eyes softened. "No, I don't believe it. I know you are trying to be fair and decent about the whole thing. But I just don't want people to think evil of me."

"If you don't believe your own accusations against me, then *why* are you telling such horrible stories to everybody? It's all coming back to *me*," I said pleadingly.

I shall never forget the look in his eyes! A look of terror and fear. The look of someone caught in a web, locked into a prison, held in a rut. "Something *makes* me say it," he said hoarsely. "Something *makes* me do it."

He promised that he would stop the gossiping for sure, and I promised him that I wouldn't discuss our family matters with anyone. With that we parted.

Two days later I had a phone call from our mutual friend, Ruth. She was absolutely drained. Rollie had kept her on the phone for two hours. It was a long-distance call, and he had ranted and raved and accused and claimed that I had so much as admitted to him at our anniversary dinner that everything he said about me was true.

I apologized to my friend and told her how sorry I was that she had to be pulled into our family affairs. Lately I seem to apologize most of the time to the whole wide world for Rollie's behavior. He even calls the school office ever so often. He usually calls in the middle of my teaching and asks for me, claiming an emergency. I race to the phone and he asks me some insignificant question. The children call me in tears. He writes the wildest letters to them and his calls rattle them.

There is something strange and eerie about this whole thing. I cannot help but feel that I am not only in the midst of a severe family squabble, but also caught by an evil supernatural power that is trying desperately to destroy all of us. Why? Why would Satan be allowed to attack us so mercilessly? Hadn't I tried to do my best ever since I became a Christian? Was it *because* I tried to serve and obey God the best I knew how that everything had gone wrong? Maybe I had misunderstood God all along. Maybe I had disobeyed God and didn't know it and now I was getting punished for my mistakes.

Several church people had warned me not to write or go out and speak so much. "When you succeed more than your husband does, it is hard on his male ego," an older woman had said to me.

Another saint said, "If you wouldn't go and run around all over the country, you wouldn't have so much trouble with your Timothy."

I would go to God in prayer, asking him to show me what I should and shouldn't do. "Trust me," he would say. "Go." Or, "Obey me and I will lead you in the right way." He is still saying it whenever I come to him and ask for clearer understanding and direction. All God says to me lately is, "Trust me, my child, trust me. I *know* what I am doing."

NOVEMBER/ *Saturday Night*

What a weekend! What a battle! Last night I hit bottom. The whole week had been a nightmare. Rollie is now at the point where he buttonholes strangers on the street and tells them his woes, along with ugly stories.

A dear friend who went to college with me came to see me. She was the first one of my church to make an attempt to ask me what *really* happened. Sure, my very own personal friends are in touch with me, but nobody else makes an effort to visit or call me. No minister has ever come to see me. No Bible worker. The only contact I have left with the church is a monthly contribution envelope they mail to me. At least they know my address.

I looked at my friend. "What is it you want to know?" I said. "Do you want the gory details, proof that I have a right to exist in my lonely apartment?"

"No," she said. "I want the truth so I can defend you. Rollie comes frequently to our house and everybody groans when they see him coming. He often manages to come at suppertime and I don't mind when he eats with us, but he has a way of ruining our meal. He seems obsessed with the theme of sex."

"Eva," I said, "I cannot believe that he is making such a fool of himself by choice. He is too intelligent and sensitive for that. There is such a frightening personality change in that man that I sometimes wonder if I am dealing with the same person.

"I am not willing to say anything against him. He is the father of my five children and I tear them down whenever I belittle him. Many times my anger and disgust get to me and I say something ugly in return when people tell me what he says. I always feel terrible afterward and ask God to forgive me. This whole thing is frightening. Please, pray for us."

She left and I hit one of the deepest depressions I had fought in months.

I also got a letter from my daughter Kathy. She is lashing out at me and I understand. I have done the same thing in times past. I lashed out at the kids when Tim moved out. I was so full of helpless frustrations and hurt. I gave them a stern lecture. Kathy said, "Mom, don't yell at us. We haven't left, Tim has."

I told them I was sorry and Kathy was right. Now Kathy is yelling at me. I understand, but it doesn't hurt less. I have the feeling that I am slowly but surely being cut to pieces. The days are bearable, as long as the principal stays out of my classroom. He is riding me lately. Maybe it's me. I know I am supersensitive and jumpy. My students seem to sense that I am upset. They have been good to me. I get very defensive when the principal gets on their case.

Last night I lay before my fake fireplace again. I hate that artificial contraption, but the gas flame warms my cold feet. Lately my hands and feet are most of the time ice cold. My stomach is a mess too. I can't eat or sleep too well. The nights are agony. My little poodle licks my face when I cry. I try hard to be sensible, but I am losing the ground under my feet and I know it.

I argued with God as I lay on the carpet. "Jesus," I said, "I want to quit. I am a total failure. I have failed as a mother, as a wife, as a teacher, and as a Christian. I don't

know why. I tried so hard to do my best since I met you.
But my best was obviously not good enough. You took
everything from me that made life worthwhile."

"Didn't you *give* me everything you had?" the Lord
reminded me gently.

I nodded into the deep silence of my dark apartment.
"Yes, Lord, I did!" I suddenly remembered and lived
through past moments as he brought them back to my
mind.

Less than a year ago I had read a book while spending
a day in bed: *Beyond Ourselves* by Catherine Marshall. I
have admired her writing for a long time, but that book
grabbed me as nothing else ever had. After I read the
whole book I reread one chapter several times: "The
Prayer of Relinquishment." That chapter points out that
we must not only give God all our talents and services,
but also be willing to give back to him, at any time, what
he gave to us in the first place—the things with which we
serve him. I knew he had given me talents to write,
speak, and sing.

"Are you willing to relinquish your speaking?" God
asked me that night.

"Yes, Lord," I said, almost a bit relieved because my
speaking had brought so much tension and a tremendous
time squeeze on me.

"Are you giving me your singing?" God said next.

"Sure, Jesus," I answered. "You know I love to sing
and have dreamed for many years of someday making a
record. But I am hardly singing anymore anyway. I give
back my voice to you."

"Will you give me your writing talent if I want it?" God
asked through my still, small voice.

I didn't answer for a long time. Writing was a way of
life for me. I had written in my mind or on paper ever
since I was very young. I won my first special writing
award while I was in special training during World War II.
When other people looked at a scene and tried to capture

a picture on canvas, I would try to paint a word picture.
To stop writing for me meant to stop living.

I struggled for hours before I finally said, "Yes, my
Lord, if you want me to stop writing, I will not write anymore. My writing is yours, too. You may have it back." I
felt *so* relieved. I had given God *everything!* It took me by
complete surprise when God asked, "Will you give me
your family, too?"

"I don't *have* to, God," I said hastily. "My family is not
mine to give, they are not a talent of mine."

"Will you give me your family?" God repeated to me.

"Lord, what do you mean by that?" I asked and felt
terribly scared. "Are you going to take them like you took
my neighbor's family when they had that terrible accident?"

"I didn't say that," God said lovingly. "I just asked you
if you are willing to give me your family."

I finally said "Yes" to that question several nights later,
after I had struggled, agonized, and argued nearly a week
with God over his puzzling request.

"I never dreamed you meant *this,*" I said yesterday to
the Lord, "but, I *did* give you everything and you took it.
You meant every word you said, didn't you?"

"Yes, I did," God said.

"Lord," I said, "I shall never speak, sing, or write
again. What an irony! The publisher just called and said
my book is selling great. They expect it to be a top best
seller. Well, as soon as the news hits the market that my
home is breaking up, it will not sell anymore. Too bad,
Lord. I had given you that book, too. And I had asked
you to make it a great blessing to many. Anyway, it's all
over! Everything is over, Lord. Can I leave now?

"I'd like to buy a one-way ticket to Europe and vanish.
My kids don't want or need me anymore. I have failed
them. Rollie will find someone else. My service for your
kingdom has brought disgrace on your name. I just want
to disappear and thus make everyone happy."

"Will you leave me, too?" Jesus said gently. "So many people have left me before when the going got rough. I was misunderstood and despised and humiliated when I walked the earth, my child. And many turned against me. Are you better than I? Are *you* going to leave me and turn on me, too?"

Tears rolled down my cheeks. "Lord," I sobbed, "what good can I do for you from now on? Can't I just leave so people will forget and your name will no longer be dishonored by this mess? After all, you are now in heaven and in joy and glory, but what do I have to look forward to? Maybe I will not be able to even go to heaven at the end. What if this whole thing is your Father's punishment upon me for some great mistake I made? Things look so dark and hopeless, Jesus, and you are back in your glory. . . ."

"Am I?" the Lord said lovingly. "Pick up the book on the coffee table and open it. I'll show you something."

I wiped my tears, sat up, turned on a light, and reached for the book. It was written by one of my favorite teachers of religion, one who taught me when I had completed my bachelor's and master's degrees a few years ago at a private college on the west coast. It was a book about the Holy Spirit.

I began to read. Some sentences caught my attention and emotions. The author said in so many words that Jesus wasn't through humiliating himself yet. Through the Holy Spirit he was still pleading, begging, and asking to be accepted and invited in. He puts himself even now at the disposal of a critical, lukewarm, and indifferent church, waiting humbly to be given his rightful place.

My tears flowed like a cleansing river. I sobbed so hard the couch shook with me. "Jesus," I said aloud into the oppressive silence, looking out the window toward the black sky, "I didn't know that you are not through with your humble role yet. You are *still* rejected most of the time, aren't you? They *still* spit in your face, shake fists at you and leave you when things go rough. Who am I to complain?

"No, Lord, I shall *not* leave you. If the rest of my life has nothing left but pain, gossip, rejection, and loneliness, I will not run away. I will stay."

DECEMBER/ *Sunday Night*

Things have begun to look up since that special Friday night last month. I should say, it got better within me, not outwardly. My external problems seemed to go from bad to worse for a while.

Financial pressure was squeezing me so much that I couldn't see my way out anymore. I promised the kids that I would bring them home for Christmas vacation, but I simply didn't have the money for three round-trip tickets. Well, I made the reservations anyhow. I told God that the money was his problem, not mine, and left the burden with him.

I also got sick. It began over Thanksgiving weekend when I went off by myself. Our former neighbors in the mountains offered me the key to their cabin. I accepted gratefully and drove up. Nobody was there. It was a lonely weekend. I would sit on their porch and look across to the cabin we had lived in for three years. All I could think was, "Why did everything go wrong? Why?"

I had brought a small precooked turkey up with me to have my own Thanksgiving dinner. I felt too nauseated to eat. I began to wonder if I was starting to get another ulcer. My doctor had already warned me last summer that it might happen.

"For others, it is just a painful thing," he had said. "But for you it could be a matter of life and death since you have only one-third of a stomach left."

It was that statement by my doctor, spoken a few months ago, that caused the final breakup of our home. I had come back from the doctor's office and written a letter to Rollie. We were past the time of normal speaking terms by then. I suggested we separate for a while until we could work things out with less heat and more maturity. Rollie didn't believe I was sick. He packed and left in a huff. He said that my stomach problem was only an excuse. I wish it were! The pain is terribly real and so is my nausea. I am still losing weight, but I know now that I will be all right. I just know it!

God is so good to me. I am overwhelmed by his care and love. The money for the flight tickets for my children came from a totally unexpected source, and on time. Mabel's friend sent it to me. She hardly knows me. She wrote me a letter and told me that God spoke to her one morning after her prayers and advised her to mail me the money. She obeyed. "It's a gift," she wrote, "not a loan. I don't want you to feel obligated in any way."

I cried with joy. "I will send the same amount of money under your name to a special mission project in Europe as soon as I can," I wrote back when I thanked her. I knew she wasn't rich, and I didn't feel right in accepting the money as a gift. Her obedience deserved a double blessing.

When I saw my doctor last week he was very stern with me. "I am expecting you in the hospital for X-rays and tests," he said without a smile. "It looks like you have gall stones. If I find any, we operate immediately."

I protested. The kids were coming home. I had a Christmas dinner to serve in my classroom. I had no time.

"You will take the time," he said grimly. He is like a father to me. "You are losing your strength rapidly, and I would rather operate before you are only skin and bones."

I drove the next afternoon, after school was out, to the

hospital. Before I went, I knelt down in my living room and asked God to do what was best. "Don't be afraid," God said. "You *are* healed."

I didn't argue. I don't argue with the Lord anymore. Ever since I promised him that I would never run from him, I just take what comes and don't question. Whatever comes, it's his problem, not mine.

I surely didn't feel healed when I got up from my knees. I was sick. My right side hurt so badly I couldn't move too well. And the thought of food caused more nausea as I drove to the hospital.

The doctor did every test under the sun. He came back with a puzzled look. "We cannot find a thing," he said. "You must have a severe case of shattered nerves." I grinned. Maybe it was my nerves, maybe it wasn't. I packed my stuff and drove back home. I am still nauseated. I still have a hard time keeping food down, but I believe God. I am healed; he said so!

I make myself eat, little bits at a time. The other day I had an emergency. I ran out of money to buy food and my refrigerator was completely empty. My paycheck hadn't come in on time. During lunch I drove to the post office to check my mailbox. I had put a small ad in a church magazine, offering autographed copies of my book for a reduced prepaid price. (My publisher lets me have my book at the wholesale price.) I have sold quite a few copies the last several months. It surely helps my finances. Every penny helps right now.

I was so sure that I would find some orders with checks in the mail. I didn't! Not one letter was in my box.

"Lord," I said, "I don't know what to do. You know I have to eat to keep my strength up. You also know how my low blood sugar acts up when I go without breakfast. It's your problem. I had to pay the bills; I also gave my tithe. The problem is yours again."

A young man walked into my art classroom that afternoon during my last class period. The class buzzed with activity and noise. He introduced himself as a map sales-man who just had been in the principal's office. The gentleman said with a German accent, "Your principal told me about you. He said you wrote a book about your experiences. I would love to read it. Do you have, by any chance, one of your books here for sale?"

Of course I did! He handed me the money and I gave him an autographed copy. We shook hands and he left with a smile.

God is so wonderful! I stopped after school at the mar-ket and bought eggs, bread, and fruit.

Ever since I let go and don't struggle or question God, as I did when it all began, he has taken my life under his control again. Though the cloud over the sun hasn't left, and the pain stays with me day and night, the apartment has become more bearable. The stillness has a new sound, too. The sound of a cricket. My little friend lives somewhere behind the refrigerator and seems to have lived here for weeks. Every night he chirps his song for hours. I go to sleep by that sound and feel comforted and less alone. Cricket-chirping is a happy childhood sound for me. It lets me forget that I live alone in a city. It re-minds me of green mountain meadows and fresh-smelling hay in a hayloft. I wake up at night to that sound and go right back to sleep again. I thank God for sending that cricket to me. He understands. I wouldn't dare tell it to anyone else; they'd think I have gone crazy. I believe he keeps the little thing alive for me. I never heard of a crick-et living for weeks in an apartment. I told my poodle not to harm the creature during the day when I am gone. I wonder what the insect lives on. I don't know too much about crickets except that they make their chirping sound with their big hind legs. I wonder if the cricket misses the outdoors. It's raining a lot. I hope the little thing is glad to be inside. And so we live together: my Lord, my poodle, my cricket, and I.

JANUARY/ *Wednesday Night*

The children have left. Christmas turned out much better
than I had dared to hope for. We didn't have many gifts
under the tree, but some of my friends came lovingly
through and sent things to the kids. Tim spent time with
us. Rollie came over for Christmas Eve. It was almost like
it always had been. He read the usual Christmas story
from the Gospel of Luke. We sang, we lit candles, we
opened presents. The form was there, the warmth had
gone. How can people who lived together for so many
years in the same house all of a sudden become total
strangers to each other? Rollie isn't the person I knew and
loved for so long. It's almost as though he brings a chill
with him when he steps into the room. He is fidgety,
nervous; his eyes never meet mine. I ache for him, but I
know I can't help him. Whatever he struggles with, this is
his warfare, not mine.

God tells me over and over to keep my hands off. I
don't argue. I don't reason anymore with Rollie either. It
is of no use.

Mabel called me a few days ago. She sounded very
upset. "Do you have special locks on your door?" she
said. "I fear for your life!" Rollie had called her again. He
had scared her with his threats against me.

I assured her that I was all right. I recognize that Rollie
is going through a terrible crisis. I pray constantly for him,
every time he comes to my mind.

It came as a total surprise to me last week when God
impressed me to file for divorce. I didn't argue with God.
I simply said, "Lord, you *know* that I don't believe in divorce. I wouldn't have stayed in my marriage as long as I
did if I could have justified divorce. I don't ever want to
question you, God, but if that is truly your will, please
send the message back to me by two or three witnesses."

I had asked for two or three witnesses at times before
in my life, whenever I had to make momentous decisions

and I wanted to make sure that I was acting by God's will alone. I knew that was biblical and God had always honored my request. I could trust him!

The first witness was Mabel. She called and sounded very disturbed. "Sis," she said haltingly, "I am supposed to tell you something from God, but I don't want to."

"What is it?" I said quickly.

"You are supposed to file for divorce. For the last three days God is giving me that message, and I have argued with the Lord and pleaded with him to be shown if it truly was his message.

"You know me well enough," she said. "I don't believe in divorce under any circumstances. That's why I stay married . . ." Mabel's voice trailed off.

"I know," I said. "How well I know! I don't believe in divorce either." And then I told her about my own request to God to give me clear signs.

"I don't know what to say," Mabel said. "I am completely shaken by the whole thing. From the human standpoint alone it's the worst time to do it now. Rollie is so upset, if he finds out what you did. . . ."

"Please don't worry," I said. "I am in God's hands and underneath are his everlasting arms. All that matters is that I obey him, and I shall do so as soon as I know for sure what his will is in the matter."

The next message came from another person I never would have expected it from: my daughter, Kathy. "Mom," she wrote, "I think it is time you file for divorce. Things cannot go on as they are now. Everytime Dad calls, he threatens that he will finally file for divorce. He never does. It keeps us in the air and uptight all the time. Get it over with—and it will also force Dad to help you financially. You cannot carry the whole load alone. If you can work things out together, you can do it after the divorce and get remarried."

Leave it to Kathy, I thought. She can be a bundle of emotions and such a handful to raise, but in times of crisis she usually ends up very sensible and mature above her age.

I talked to Tim when he came to visit me. We had become rather good friends lately. "Mom, you'll do everyone a favor," he said. "Maybe it will shake Dad up. He is stupid to let a woman like you go. I can't understand his thinking at all." Tim's kind words felt like oil on my wounds, and I sat and cried after he left.

I decided to call a lawyer friend. He was on the school board, a church member of my former church, and greatly respected in the community. I called for an appointment. The secretary asked me about the nature of my request. I choked and coughed, ". . . mmm, oh, well, about . . . family matters." I could not bring myself to say the word *divorce.*

The lawyer looked at me when I told him the situation. "You owe it to your children and yourself to protect the family financially and otherwise," he said.

"Could I file for legal separation?" I said to him. "I don't believe in divorce."

"Yes, you can," he said kindly. "But I advise you against it. It's double the cost when you want later to get a divorce, and you go through the emotional trauma twice. After all, either one of you might want to get remarried someday."

I shook my head. "I'll *never* remarry. I don't believe in it, and furthermore I am sure that I'll never take any risk of being hurt again. However, I know that Rollie will never stay alone, so we'd better do it right and give him the freedom he needs."

The lawyer set up the papers. "Are you asking for any financial support?" he asked.

"I don't want any money for myself, but I do request that he takes the responsibility for Peter. That boy needs a father so badly. I want to force my husband to look after him! I'll take care of the girls."

The lawyer saw me to the door. "I am so sorry that it

had to happen to your family," he said. "You have been looked up to almost as a model family in the community. You seemed to be so solid in every way. Every week in church, active in church doings, much respected as a teacher, your children all educated in church schools . . ."

"I know," I said. "So many people tell me that they would never have believed that this could have happened to us. Well, it happened!"

As I walked away I turned around and said, "Be very gentle and patient with Rollie, will you? Don't pressure him. Let him think it through and sign whenever he sees fit."

He smiled at me. He understood.

Today I saw Rollie. I had driven to Tim's place to bring him a birthday present. Tim wasn't home, so I sat in the car and waited. Rollie drove up and obviously didn't know what to do. He finally stepped out of his car to speak to me.

"Your lawyer has contacted me," he said. "Why did you do it?"

"Because I believe God wanted me to do it," I said. "I think it will help all of us to draw some clear lines."

"I have gone through some horrible weeks," Rollie said.

"I know," I answered. "God has shown me that you hit bottom!"

"How strange that you would say that," Rollie said, and his eyes softened.

"Shall I tell you what your struggle is?" I said to him.

"Tell me," he said. "I want to know what you know about me."

"Remember in your past how often we discussed it together and I told you that someday you would find out that you cannot solve everything in life with your own sharp intellect? You are finding it out right now, aren't you? You cannot manipulate, scare, reason, argue, threaten, rage, or force this whole thing. You are against a brick wall. You have finally come to the end of your own resources and tricks. So far in your life you always got your way, one way or another. By refusing to do *anything* you force others to do it for you. And then you can avoid or blame them. This time it backfired. Rollie, you have come to the end because God wants to show you that *he* has the answers. You don't! Maybe for once you should let God have *all* of you and not set up conditions for him. You cannot bargain with God, Rollie, as you have all along. It's either *all* of you or nothing. You have to give him *everything*. Whatever you keep, you will lose!"

"You are right," Rollie said and walked away.

FEBRUARY/ *Thursday Night*

Life is getting busier again. I would never have dared to dream of it, but I have so many calls for speaking engagements and so many letters coming in, I don't know how to handle the mail on top of my teaching load anymore. And I thought I'd never speak again! God is so loving and tender. First, he brings his children to the place where they let go and hand everything over to him; then he gives it all back to us, more beautiful than ever. I didn't believe that it could possibly happen, but it did. God *is* using me in spite of my problems.

It began last fall with a visit to a church where Corrie ten Boom spoke. She introduced me to the church secretary and the assistant pastor. Karen, who lived in the same apartment complex, was with me. She drove me there. She had a couple of my books in her car and left them with the church people. They called back a week later and asked if I could give a short testimony at their Sunday morning service, which was televised. I agreed.

I shall never forget that particular Sunday morning. I walked down the aisle to the platform beside the senior pastor, who didn't know me at all. He had spoken only a few sentences to me before the service. He informed me politely but firmly that I had no longer than five to seven minutes for my speech. He needed the rest of the time to get his message across sufficiently to the people.

I nodded. I felt dazed, numb, empty. I didn't know what I would say or if I could even open my mouth, I hurt so deeply.

The church was beautiful. One side was built completely of glass. Water fountains gushed in the sunlight. The organ played softly. We walked up the red carpeted stairs to the pulpit. And I said in my heart, "Lord, this is like a dream. It's my swan song. How kind of you to make my final appearance so beautiful. I shall never forget it. Thank you, and please do the speaking. I have no words in me!"

Before I was prepared for it, the minister motioned for me to speak. I am not sure what I said. All I know is that suddenly I looked at my watch and I had spoken twelve minutes. The audience was weeping. I wondered if the minister was mad at me. He didn't seem to be, and he preached a good sermon.

In the second service which followed an hour later, I gave a different testimony. When I had finished, something strange happened. The minister got up and called me back to the mike. He asked the audience to stand, then he said, "I have never done this before, but the Lord has impressed me to lay my hand upon her and anoint her for God's service." Then he laid one hand on my shoulder and prayed that God would use me, his handmaiden, for a worldwide ministry.

My knees shook when the audience and both of us sat down and the choir began to sing. I leaned over and whispered, "*Why* did you do that?"

He shrugged his shoulders, "I really don't know! I felt that God was telling me to do it."

I looked across the sea of faces below me and out the

big glass windows, up into the sun-filled blue sky. "Lord," I said in my heart, "the man is wrong. If he only *knew,* he would never have done it, never! It's because he doesn't know anything about me that he prayed that prayer. This isn't the beginning of a ministry, this is the *end.* You didn't tell him to do that, Jesus, did you? You would never make fun of me, even though I deserved it."

I agonized before God that afternoon in my silent apartment. I asked God why the whole thing had to hap-pen. Why did he let me be shown up so badly when I finally had come to the place of total surrender and will-ingness to live in absolute obscurity?

God didn't explain it all, he just said, "Trust me, my child, I know what I am doing. I shall do great things through you."

From that Sunday on, the calls began to come in. The readers' mail increased, too, since the book was selling so surprisingly well. By January it had made the top ten on the religious best-seller list. Now my telephone keeps ringing. I finally had to hook up an answering service be-cause I am gone most of the time. During the day I teach, in the evenings and on weekends I speak—in clubs, in churches, at banquets—and I enjoy it while it lasts. I am fully aware that it will be only for a little while longer, and then I won't be asked anymore. As soon as the news spreads that I am in the process of divorce, the religious community will drop me. Since I am not willing to speak on anything else but how I love God and America, the secular society will have no use for me either. So that will be it!

It doesn't matter that much to me. But it's a joy while it is still going on. People are so good to me and assure me over and over that God has spoken to them through my words. I smile and thank them, but I always wonder what they would say if they knew about my divorce. God has given me clear orders not to talk about it at least not at the present time, never to mention my family problems from the pulpit, never to bring it up unless I am asked. It's almost as though I am in another world when I step up to a mike. The dark cloud lifts. I tune in to God and forget everything else. Nothing matters at that moment but that I say *only* what he wants me to say.

I never speak with notes. I tried it. It doesn't work for me. I understand why God wants it this way. I must learn to depend on him alone, on nothing or nobody else. God knows me so well. I am his unruly kid. If I were permitted to plan ahead or outline a speech, I could easily believe that I was able to do the whole thing by myself. I know better than that. If he lets me go but for *one* moment, I break. I am walking such a fine line between victory and defeat right now, it would be frightening if I couldn't trust my Lord.

The problems haven't really gone away. They pile up like mountains at times. My speaking has eased the financial pressure, though, and I praise the Lord for that. I have not set a speaker's fee. I just accept whatever anyone gives or doesn't give me. I never know what to expect. The largest churches will often hand me the smallest amount or nothing at all. A tiny group will surprise me with a generous love offering. I never know and I don't worry about it. I take it all as out of God's hand anyway.

I was able to pay back the money Mabel's friend had sent for my children's Christmas trips. She agreed to have it sent to Europe. I have set up a system by which we are able to convert dollars into West German marks. That money then buys paper and ink, right in the heart of a Communist country, to print Bibles and literature for my people. My tithe money has gone for years for that purpose, and no other.

Christians are beginning to help me a bit. I can't talk about it too much. The less it is known, the safer it is for those who are involved on the other end. My heart goes out to those suffering Christians behind the Iron Curtain. If I think I have problems, they have more. At least I have my Bible and am free to read it. How would I have made it through the last year without the comfort of God's Word? At times I would read Psalm 37 twice a day. God gave me that Scripture as a special message one day, shortly before our home broke. I have been clinging to several texts in it and claim his promises daily.

"He shall give thee the desires of thine heart," and "He shall bring forth thy righteousness as the light, and thy judgment as the noonday" (Psalm 37:4, 6).

The greatest desire my heart knows is the assurance of salvation for my whole family, Rollie included. Tina and Tim are not yet Christians. My three younger children have their ups and downs. One letter reaches out, the next letter lashes out. And I am caught in the middle of their frustrations and search.

Rollie's slander campaign is often more than I can humanly handle, especially since God does not permit me to defend myself, not even to my children. Sometimes I begin to wonder if I am innocent or guilty of everything he says. Maybe I don't know my own heart. Maybe I am a freak and don't know it. What if it is true and I am not normal, as he suggests? All I can do is pray, and I seem to do that every free moment I have. "Lord," I beg over and over, "show me what I need to know, please.

"If I am guilty, show it to me and wash me clean. If I am innocent in your eyes, defend and clear me. Let me not bring shame to your name."

MARCH/ *Monday Evening*

Rollie has not signed the divorce papers yet. I called the lawyer, who said he did what I had asked him to do. He didn't push or urge Rollie; he just waited patiently for him to decide.

I did one thing. My bank account is no longer a joint one, and I have informed Rollie's bank that I am no longer responsible for any of his debts. A small notice in the local paper has announced the same thing. That took a big load off my shoulders. I know that I have to be financially responsible for my children's sake. Rollie has to learn to be the same.

The last few weeks are overshadowed by struggle again, a new inner struggle. I believe that God is telling me not to sign my teaching contract for next year. I literally almost fell off the couch when he told me the first time. I lay flat on the carpet because my knees felt shaky. It's my favorite position in which to pray, anyway. I can't look any place but up when I am on my back.

"Lord," I said, "I'd better make sure I am hearing you *right*. This not only involves *my* future but my *children's* future, too. I don't need a big salary to live on, but you *know* what it costs to educate the children. Tim is now back in college, too, and once in a while I have to help out when his car breaks down or some extra bills pile up for him. I have four children in school, Lord."

"I know," God said. "I put them there. I also took care of every bill you had to pay."

"What do you want me to do if I am supposed to quit teaching, Lord? What will my students do if I leave? I am needed where I am, or am I not?" I asked.

"You are needed more in other places," God answered. "I want you to begin speaking and writing for me full-time after this school year is over. Do it the same way your Tante Corrie does it."

I was so overwhelmed I went to see Corrie ten Boom. I thanked God that she was in the area for a short time.

"Tante Corrie," I said timidly, "God has told me to quit my teaching job and serve him full-time, just like you. What do you think I should do?"

"My child," she said, "if God tells you to go, you go. If he calls you into his service, you obey. That is simple, isn't it?"

"Yes, Tante," I said, "it is simple for you, but I have several children to support."

I had never spoken with her about my divorce, but I knew that she knew about it.

"Is God not able to support you and your children?" she asked, and her childlike eyes gave me a puzzled look. She couldn't see my perplexity at all.

I changed the subject. "Tante Corrie, tell me how you handle your ministry." I knew the story already but I wanted to hear it again, to be assured that it could be done the way she did it.

She had never asked for a speaker's fee, ever. She never offered her services. God showed her where and when to go. And he took care of her needs. She had traveled as "God's tramp" for more than thirty years.

I had the same instructions to follow that way, but I had a different family situation. Corrie had never married, and she traveled with a secretary. I was married, in the process of a divorce, and the mother of five children. I was also alone—to answer the mail, to make arrangements, to travel, to sell my books after the meetings. It was all getting too big for me to handle and I knew it.

"Corrie, you have Ellen to help you. I have nobody," I said, stalling again.

"So we pray that God will send you an Ellen, yes?" she said in her Dutch accent. Her eyes twinkled; her hands squeezed mine tightly. "God does not call us into failure and confusion. He makes provisions for everything."

We prayed together before I left and my heart was at peace. I would resign.

My principal gave me an incredulous look when I announced my decision to him the following day. "I hope you know what you are doing," he said gruffly. "You know it takes a lot of speaking to bring in what you earn now. And if your plans fail, you have a slim chance of getting back into your present position."

I knew what I stood to lose. The devil reminded me over and over of what I had: a life tenure in the district, the position of Master Teacher, training students from the nearby college; the following year I was to reach the highest level of pay on the scale. With the just-voted cost-of-living increase, I had a substantial raise coming. My financial problems would for once be solved. For the first time in my life, for as far back as I could remember, I would have enough to live on.

Tim looked at me and shook his head in utter bewilderment when I told him. "Mother, are you using your head at all in this? You know how many teachers are walking the streets right now, unemployed. And you are throwing away a secure, respected position without being forced to do so? If they fired you or had you laid off it would be different. But you are resigning by your free choice and will. Use your head, Mother. The kids need you for several years to come. Peter is only fourteen years old."

"I know, Tim," I said, feeling helpless to explain it sensibly. "I understand what you are saying and I appreciate your concern. But I cannot go by my head. Son, I must go by my heart and by what God shows me. You see, Christians cannot lean on their own understanding, they must first obey God."

"Are you *sure* God wants you to do that?" Tim said.

"*I am sure*," I said. "I am very sure."

I wasn't as sure as I sounded. I went back to God again and again. "Lord, what if I am making a mistake? What if it isn't your will after all? What if I misunderstood your directions? Everyone is telling me that I am crazy; even good Christian friends warn me that I am presumptuous, Lord. You know that I love to teach and I love my students. You know how upset some of them are because I am leaving the school. God, what will happen to my own children if I take more security away from them? They have so little left."

I agonized, worried, cried, prayed, and pleaded until I felt too weary to think anymore. I knew every reason why I shouldn't leave my job. I knew also why my future plans

could not work, at least not as long as my home breakup
is not mended.

I have no assurance from God that Rollie and I will
ever get back together here on this earth. I believe that
we shall all be together in heaven. For me, that is
enough. For my future work, it isn't. People will not understand. I know what my common sense tells me, how
my intellect reasons and what my friends advise me to
do. But I believe that God has told me to get out and
serve him more fully. And I will obey him, even if it
makes no sense to me or anyone else right now. I need
his peace more than I need security.

APRIL/ *Monday Night*

The last month has been a whirlwind which has left me
slightly dazed.

When I counted how often I had spoken, I added up
thirty-seven different appointments. Of course, I couldn't
have done it if it had not been for spring vacation at
school. I spent the whole two weeks in the Midwest. God
has a way of bringing invitations and coordinating them
into a speaking tour which leaves me filled with adoration
and love for him.

If I ever could have believed that I was subject to
chance, luck, fate, or circumstances, the last month has
proved to me beyond the shadow of a doubt that God *is*
in control of everything in his children's lives. That was
never more evident than when little Mary called. She is
the church secretary at the church where the minister
prayed for me last fall. I came home from teaching one
afternoon and began to listen to my recorded phone messages. The first message was from Mary. "Please call back
as soon as you can," she said. "We have an emergency."

I called back immediately. Indeed they did have an
emergency! The minister's wife was in charge of a na-

tional convention for their church women. Mary had
scheduled Corrie ten Boom as their key speaker. The arrangements had been made one and a half years before
the set date. The convention was only weeks away when
Corrie's agency called to cancel because she was tied up
with the filming of *The Hiding Place* in Holland. Mary
sounded shaky and upset. "Could you possibly speak in
her place?" she said. "We don't want to make you feel
like second fiddle."

"That doesn't bother me at all," I said. "But let me
check my calendar. If God wants me to do it, the date
will be open. If not, he will send you someone else. I
don't believe in canceling previous commitments in order
to do something else, even if it would be for something
bigger or better."

The date was free. I had appointments before and after
the date, but that particular evening was not filled yet.

I spent some anxious hours before the Lord as the
night came closer. "Lord," I asked, "how can a former
Nazi girl speak to several thousand church women, mostly
of Dutch origin? And in place of their beloved fellow-
country-woman Corrie ten Boom, on top of that? How
can I get away with it? They might boo me off the stage
before I am finished, and I couldn't blame them. I am
afraid that it's going to be one big flop and humiliation
for me. But I'll do it because you asked me to do it."

"Trust me," God said. "I have a big surprise for you. I
know what I am doing."

The convention hall was packed with people. A sea of
stony faces looked toward the platform; not one smile encouraged me when I began to speak.

I knew that the people had every reason to be disappointed because Corrie wasn't there. They didn't know
me, and when I opened my mouth for the first sentence I
spoke with a German accent.

Thirty-five minutes later I said the last sentence and
watched several thousand people rise to give me a

standing ovation. It took me a while to comprehend that
they clapped and smiled for me. I fought hard to keep my
proper composure and the Lord said to me, "I told you
that I had a surprise for you."

I smiled and waved at the audience and tried to walk
off the platform. I couldn't. People thronged me from every side. Some had tears in their eyes. I was hugged,
squeezed, kissed, and showered with Christian love until
Mary came to rescue me. She nudged me over to the
book table where lines of people waited for an autograph.
It was long past midnight when I finally got back to my
apartment. I could just picture the Lord smiling. We
talked to each other as I drove home in the darkness of
the late night down deserted streets and quiet freeways.

"Ask Mary to work with you after the school year is
over," the Lord said after I had thanked him over and
over for the success of the evening and for Mary's
prayerful, kind help during those hours. Mary is tiny in
stature, slim, with a head full of short, gray hair that
stands in sharp contrast to her young face and childlike
blue eyes. She is such a dear person, and efficient in
handling many matters I have had no previous experience
with.

"Lord, I have no security or extra money," I said.
"Mary has worked in her position for the last ten years.
She is the minister's right arm in that church. He might
get very upset with me and with her if she leaves. And
Mary might not even consider working under such shaky
conditions as I have to offer to her."

"Ask her anyway and tell her the truth about everything, even your family problems," the Lord said to me.

It took a while before I had the nerve to broach the
subject with Mary. I called her one fall evening and asked
her to have dinner with me. While we ate, I told her what
God had said to me. "Please understand it correctly—I
have no worldly security to offer," I said to her. "I am
going into my new work against better judgment and my

friends' advice. I have no money yet, but my first royalty check is coming and I am sure that my husband will try very hard to get half of that check in our divorce settlement. He is slinging mud against not only me but also anyone who associates with me. You might become part of a very embarrassing campaign, and I am sure you don't deserve that. I can assure you of nothing but the fact that as long as I eat, you do. If I go hungry, you might be hungry too. I would have never dared to ask you in the first place, but for the simple reason that God told me to ask you, and I don't argue with God anymore. I just obey. Please pray about it and understand that I put no pressure on you. We stay friends and I will respect you as much as before if you say 'no.' I expect you to do so, if you have any common sense."

Mary didn't say "no." She said "yes" when she called me back. "Don't worry about my eating," she laughed her mischievous little laugh. "I have lived with empty cupboards before. When I went to college, I often had only one lone tea bag in the 'fridge. I have lived for weeks on tomato soup mixed with water during my youthful past. The insecurity doesn't scare me. I would like to work with you."

Already Mary has started to help me whenever she is free to do so. She sometimes drives with me to evening meetings and sets up the book table. She also arranged to have one of my messages recorded before a live audience and put on a cassette. It is unbelievable how many of those cassettes are selling. Someone had told me that speakers' cassettes simply don't sell. So I was very hesitant about entering into such a new venture. So far God is doing the impossible again: the tape is selling as well as the book. I feel so very humble and grateful to God that he *is* using me and my book in spite of my present difficulties.

I had a call the other day which encouraged me

greatly. It was from a young man in Missouri. "You are hard to find," he said. "My name is David. I am calling from a telephone booth, because my parents wouldn't understand what I am doing. The telephone operator looked for you all over the country and she finally got me your number."

"What can I do for you, David?" I said politely.

"I have to tell you what happened to me," he said. "I saw your book in a bookstore and the cover looked appealing. I have always been interested in World War II stories. I read your book and I thought it was a very exciting narrative. When I finished it, I laid it down and realized that Jesus Christ was all over me. I knew I had to make a decision. I did! I asked him into my heart right then and there, and I also asked him to give me a sign that he had heard me. I asked him to let me find you and talk to you. It took hard work and time and effort to get your telephone number, but God answered my prayer!"

The young man bubbled on and on with so much joy and excitement that I just sat and listened. I marveled at God's love and care for his human children. The boy couldn't know that he not only found my telephone number by a miracle but he called at the precise moment to find me home. Seldom did I answer my phone. I was either gone or so busy with my mail that I let my recorded message do the answering. The recording would have been like a bucket of cold water upon David's joy and eagerness to share—and God knew it! So I was home and picked up the phone. I listened patiently. I prayed with the newborn babe in Christ. I told the boy to ask God to lead him into the right church fellowship, and I gave him my address so he could write to me. I want to stay in contact with him.

When I put the receiver down, I laid my head on my arms and cried. "God," I sobbed, "why did I have to lose my own children in order to lead other young people to you? Send other Christians to my own children then; that's all the favor I dare to ask in return for what I am trying to do for other parents' kids."

"Trust me," God said again. "I will do what you ask, and more!"

JUNE/ *Thursday Night*

Life is stranger than fiction. It's like a dream, a puzzling dream, and I can't wake up and shake the burden of it.

School is over. I cleaned out my desk. Now it's waiting for the next teacher, and I am free.

They had a farewell luncheon for me. The principal and the faculty took me to a fancy restaurant and gave me cards and a gift and made some speeches. The principal's remarks gave me much to think about.

"I envy you," he said. "Maybe we all do. You have the courage to do what most of us have dreamed of doing but never had the courage for. We all have our secret dreams, what we really want to do with our lives, but have never dared to step out and do it. Our paycheck and security seem more important than our secret ambitions. You dare to take the risk and do *your* thing. We wish you luck!"

I didn't try to explain that I wasn't doing my own thing. I was obeying God. Most of the teachers weren't even church members and certainly not Christians. My principal did attend church, the church I had walked out of last summer. He figured that anyone was crazy who kept up a two-way communication with God. And I was the last one who could have convinced him otherwise.

Wasn't my broken home clear evidence that God and I had parted ways? He could envy me that I had the daring and irresponsibility and intestinal fortitude to walk out of situations I didn't want any longer, but nobody could have convinced him that God and I were still on speaking terms and that I might even be acting under God's orders.

He knew the format of true religion and he kept it. He and his wife attended church every week. He also belonged to many church and community organizations. He stayed so busy that he said to his wife on Monday mornings, "I'll see you next Friday night!"

I knew this because he had told me so himself. He also had assured me over and over that he hated his job. It was very obvious anyway, and the students knew it, too. They made it torture for him and he for them, but he would stick it out—until retirement. He thought he would do everything he ever wanted to do after retirement. "He might not make it until retirement," his wife had once said to me. "He is so often sick and will not slow down or take a proper rest, ever. And he isn't eating properly, either. Well, if it is God's will . . ."

If it was God's will? Would it be _God's_ will if a man dropped dead before his retirement because he overworked himself in a job he hated but chose to keep for security's sake?

Well, I am glad I don't have to worry about other people's problems. I have enough of my own. And I try to sort out my own life.

I have to move, finalize plans for the coming school year for my children, decide if I want to sign a contract to write another book, and set up the structure for a ministry. I also need to pay a salary to Mary, who will soon begin to work for me full-time.

This is a handful for someone like me who learned how to drive a car only three years ago. And I hardly ever wrote a check before my home broke up. It wasn't by choice that I stayed dependent on someone else's driving and banking for so long, but what could I do? Rollie insisted that we couldn't afford a second car and that I was

not capable of learning how to drive or handle money.
So I handed him my paycheck. I went along with him for
the sake of *harmony*. I had learned to wait for rides ever
since we had come to America. In Europe I had used
public transportation, but the USA is car-oriented. Mercy
on anyone who doesn't own or drive a car in this affluent
land. It's sheer agony!

Well, my plight was ended when we moved to the
mountains. I simply had to drive my own car to work.
Rollie wasn't about to get up every morning to drive me
to work unless he had to go to school, and he tried to
avoid early morning classes, if possible. He is a person
who loves to stay up at night but has a hard time with
early rising. Well, people are different: some are night
fireflies, others are early birds. I seem to be both—not by
choice, but by necessity.

I shall never forget the day I took the test to get my
driver's license. The whole family was sure that I wouldn't
pass. They teased and laughed about my nervousness.
Rollie assured me that the highway department would
begin to plant rubber trees if I ever got behind a wheel. I
laughed and tried to hide my tears. Jokes can be so cruel
when a person is as scared as I was. When I was actually
driving, with the examiner beside me my hands shook
and I made every possible mistake. The officer shifted
uneasily behind his seat belt. When we finally came back
to a halt at the motor vehicle department, he looked up
and said, "Look, lady, I cannot believe that you will be as
lousy a driver as you just demonstrated. You are obviously so nervous that you can't think straight. I'll pass you
anyway if you promise me you'll be a very careful
driver."

I cried with joy and thanked him in deep-felt gratitude.
I promised him I would be a cautious and skillful driver. I
have kept my word. So far, I have never had a ticket or
an accident, not even since I got my little sports car a few

months ago. That little MG can be such a temptation to speed, but I know better. God gave me that car and I'd better take good care of it, even though it *was* built for faster speeds than 55 mph. I hardly touch the gas pedal and the little thing roars away.

The way I got that car is another funny and beautiful story of how God cares and answers. I drove only cars with automatic shifts up to the time the energy crisis hit. During the worst of that crisis, we were allowed to buy gasoline only on alternate days. With my heavy after-work and weekend speaking schedule, I was in a tight spot to keep my appointments on the odd days when I couldn't buy gas.

I went to the Lord about it. "Lord," I said, "I need a car with better gas mileage or I can't keep all my engagements for you."

He sent me to a Christian friend who was a car dealer. Rob looked out the window and pointed to a little gold car on the lot. "I have just the car for you," he said. "It will give you twenty-eight miles per gallon."

We went out to look at it and I saw the manual shift. I shook my head and said, "I can't shift and I am too dumb to learn such technical things!"

Rob said, "You can learn it if you want to; it's not that hard."

"Let me pray about it," I stalled. "That thing scares me."

"OK, I'll give you a couple hours," he said. "I can't hold it any longer. Too many people are after small cars right now. Call me back."

I called back after I had prayed about it. "Rob," I said, "I'll take the car if you drive it into my garage space. I can't drive it home myself."

He laughed and brought me the sports car and drove the car with the automatic shift back to the lot.

I went by bicycle to work the following mornings. On

the weekend I drove the sports car to a side road near the apartment and practiced shifting. I couldn't do it. I finally stopped at the side of the road, wiped the sweat and tears off my face, and said aloud to God, "Lord, you *told* me to get this car, so you will have to drive it. I can't! You have promises and gifts for *every* human need in your word. The only reason that I couldn't find a Bible promise for gear shifting is that there were no cars when the Bible was written, otherwise you would have put one in. I will just have to claim a new gift from you: the gift of shifts!"

Then I started the car again and said, "You shift with your hand over mine, please." He did! He has been shifting *ever* since. And I let him do the driving, too. It's easier that way, for me and others.

He is also helping me to write my own checks now, and balance a bank account. He is teaching me so many new things. I learned to deal with state offices about sales taxes and other commercial things. Since I am selling my books and cassettes after meetings, I need these licenses. He is showing me how to repair things in the home, things which had stayed broken as long as I expected Rollie to fix them. He seldom found the time. I fill out applications and other insurance forms that I would never have dared to touch before because I thought I couldn't do such things, *ever*.

I can! A woman can do many things if she *has* to. I found that out during these last ten months while I have been living by myself.

I have begun to feel more sure of myself and my ability to cope with life than I *ever* felt before. I have, for sure, nobody but the Lord to depend upon now, especially since I have no more regular paychecks coming. But I carry a deep peace and assurance in me. I know not only *what* I believe; I know *whom* I believe. That is surely enough for me!

JULY/ *Tuesday Morning*

Rollie signed the divorce papers shortly after I finished up the school year. It took me completely by surprise because he had stalled for so long. I was sure that he was waiting for my royalty check to come in. Our state laws favor the equal division of property and money in case of divorce. Since he possesses nothing and I have money coming, the law is in his favor.

I couldn't figure out what changed his mind. It was obviously not the Lord, because his slander hasn't stopped but has gotten worse since he signed the papers. I will know that the Holy Spirit has gotten through to Rollie's heart only when he stops raging and comes and asks forgiveness for his slander. Even if he actually believes what he says, God's Spirit of love will have to convict him that God's children are *never* allowed to gossip, even if sin is truly evident in another's life. Rollie has no evidence, but he will use anything, any word I say or write to him, to fabricate some new stories. He has a mastermind, and that's why I was so puzzled about his sudden cooperation.

I got my answer when I visited my lawyer personally to discuss the date of the court settlement. "What happened?" I asked my lawyer friend. "How did we get the signature all of a sudden?"

"I don't know," he said. "He called me one day and asked if your offer was still on."

"Which offer?" I said.

"That you wouldn't demand any financial aid from him except the responsibility for your younger son, Peter," the lawyer answered. "I told him you hadn't changed a word on the agreement," my friend continued, "and your husband came over almost immediately to sign the papers. He showed signs of great relief after he had signed, and was most cooperative in every way. He asked me to represent him in court, too, since the case is going to be un-contested."

The light hit me all at once. Rollie must have found out, either through Tim or Heidi, that I had resigned my secure position and was, as far as he could see, unemployed. That made him by law the provider for the entire family. Now I could sue him for alimony for all three children and myself.

I couldn't help but smile a bit. "Poor Rollie," I said to the lawyer. "I think I know now why he signed so fast, before I could change my mind. I have resigned my job and plan to go into full-time writing and speaking. It must have scared him no end."

The lawyer gave me the same incredulous look I always get when I tell people what I just have done. Then we talked over the divorce procedure. I also paid him my share of the lawyer's fee. "Let me know if Rollie doesn't pay his share," I said. "I will pay both fees if need be. I don't want you to have any unpaid bills on my account."

"Don't worry, he'll pay," he said. "He is too eager to get this thing settled in his favor while he is able to do so. I myself will have to point out to you that you are taking the greater risk in this whole deal, and you wouldn't have to at all. The law is now completely on your side, since you have no job and your husband works steadily."

"I know," I said, "but I believe that God will provide for us. The reason that I even ask Rollie to care for Peter is more psychological than monetary. Peter needs a dad so badly. My baby is suffering the most under the breakup. He needs a father's attention more than a mother's at the present."

I cried on my way home.

God had been so good. I had moved to another mountain home and it is beautiful. I have never lived in such luxury before. It is a condominium in A-line form, with three levels. The front is all glass, and I can touch the evergreen trees when I walk out to the deck. The place is exquisitely furnished. Mary has her office and living quarters downstairs. The middle level is a spacious living and dining room area and a super-modern kitchen. The upper level is my "hayloft." I have my own bath up there, and my bed and my desk, and I look at trees and mountains whenever I write.

I should say, when I am *trying* to write. Things are not going well for me. I have come to a dead end within myself again. I think I know what is causing it. It is slowly sinking into my mind that the whole ugly dream is for real. It's *me* who is getting a divorce. It's *me* who has two children in the Midwest who refuse to come home for the summer because they may be caught in conflict. Tina isn't writing at all. Heidi is in Colorado. I sent her to a special mountain camp since we couldn't find a job for her nearby. Tim comes to see me occasionally. He and his girl friend still live together.

For nearly a year now I have carried the ball. I smile a lot in public. I seldom lose my composure when I am with someone else, even if it is my children or Mary. I write many encouraging letters from day to day.

I cry when I am alone and I am crying more and more. I am suddenly so tired that I can hardly get up in the morning. I feel completely listless and the thought of food repulses me. I make myself eat, little bits at a time. I go through the motions of daily living, but they are motions only. I am dead inside, burned out. I live in the mountains and I can't see the beauty anymore. It's like mildew over my soul. I am on my way to a nervous breakdown and I know it.

My last speaking appointment did not help. Someone from my former church called from New York state. The bad news had obviously not traveled that far yet. I don't get too many invitations from my former denomination. They've dropped me like a hot potato without asking me for *my* side of the story. I wouldn't have said too much in my defense, but I would have asked them to pray about the matter. The Holy Spirit could have shown them what they needed to know. They never asked—it's human nature to avoid sensitive issues. I have become at least an issue in question for that church, and they try to ignore the whole thing. I was surprised when the call came in. They wanted me to speak at a camp meeting. I asked the Lord what he wanted me to do. He told me to go, and I went.

They had assured me that I had a light speaking schedule and enough time between meetings to write. I told them that I had signed a contract and had a deadline to meet.

One of their main speakers canceled at the last moment, and I ended up speaking several times a day. I not only spoke for the adults, but in the youth and children's divisions. Whenever I spoke, the people packed the place. My heart ached. Common church folk everywhere seem to be so hungry for a practical, everyday approach to Christian living. I never had any other burden but to lift up Jesus. Now I spoke *only* of him. The response was gratifying to my tired body and soul. People assured me over and over that they could see Jesus more clearly at the end of their camp session.

I was urged to stay for the Spanish camp, too. I did. I hadn't previously done much speaking through an interpreter, and I learned a lot. One has to speak without feedback from the audience—or rather, only with delayed feedback. I couldn't tell if I was getting through at all. The people couldn't speak to me after the meetings, but they smiled a lot!

God sent me some extra encouragement through the manager of the church's bookstore. "You proved something that I haven't seen in thirty-seven years of my work in the book field," he said to me. "It is a well-known fact that sales of a speaker's book never go far above a hundred copies or so. You broke every record. We had to fly another shipment in, and the Spanish-speaking people are buying your book even though they cannot read it in English themselves. They want their children to read it for them."

I smiled and nodded. I left at the end of the two weeks completely exhausted. The moist summer heat and the mosquitoes had worn me out. I nearly crawled off the plane when I finally got back.

Mary stood at the gate. She took one look at me and said, "They worked you half to death! I was afraid of that. I'll never let you speak for them again, and I won't let you travel alone anymore. People have to stop taking such advantage of you. If we can't keep you alive, you will not be much good for anybody. You look terrible."

I know I look terrible. I feel terrible, too. I am turning bitter inside and I can't stop myself. I am even too tired to try. I pray and I plead and I feel darkness close in on me.

"God, is this the end of everything? I thought I obeyed you. I resigned from my teaching job. Now I can't write. I can't go and speak anymore. I can't sleep or eat. I can't carry on any longer. If I get sick, I am not even covered with medical insurance. I called Mary out of a secure position and now I am not so sure I will need her. God, what did I do wrong?"

AUGUST/ *Sunday Morning*

How can four short weeks produce such a drastic difference in a human life?

A few weeks ago I felt like dying, giving up, having a nervous breakdown. This morning I feel like a newborn person, ready to face the world with a renewed mind and new courage. It all began with a visit from Colleen, a missionary girl who works for the Lord in Rome. She was home on furlough, and we invited her to spend some days in our mountain home for rest and relaxation. She expressed her gratitude by leaving three Watchman Nee

books between two marble bookends. We found it all in
front of our fireplace after she had left to go back to Italy.

Since I couldn't bring myself to work on my book
manuscript anyway, I began to read these books. They
were laborious but most fascinating reading for me. I had
read shorter writings by Nee before, but never whole volumes.

The concepts in *The Spiritual Man* helped me greatly.
What insight, what depth! That precious Chinese brother
in Christ was taught by God. I had no doubt about it. He
also had some answers for me which I urgently needed. I
never expected to find them in those books when I began
to read.

It wasn't until I had worked myself through to volume
III that I found a surprising new concept. Watchman Nee
speaks there about the mind as a battlefield where the
Holy Spirit and evil spirits battle for control. He points out
that a born-again Christian may have a new life and new
heart but an old head (mind). The Bible teaches clearly
that we must be transformed by the renewal of the mind
(Romans 12:2). Nee also proves that born-again believers
can have their minds attacked and controlled by evil
spirits.

"The head [of the believer], for instance, may be
teeming with all kinds of uncontrollable thoughts,
imaginations, impure pictures, wanderings, and confused
ideas. His memory may suddenly fail; his power of concentration may be weakened, he may be obsessed by
prejudices which arise from unknown sources, his
thoughts may be retarded as if his mind were being
chained, or he may be flushed with wild thoughts with re-
solve increasingly in his head. The Christian may find he
is powerless to regulate his mental life and make it obey
the intent of his will. He forgets innumerable matters both
large and small. He carries out many improper actions
without knowing why and without so much as investigat-
ing the reason. Physically he is quite healthy, but mentally

he does not comprehend the explanation for these symptoms. Currently many saints encounter these mental difficulties, but without knowing why."

The author then proceeds to tell why such things can happen to even a born-again Christian. He explains that God never governs the mind of man. He gave his creatures a free will. (The will, intellect, and emotions are the three functions of man's soul.) God, therefore, intended for man to control himself. Man decides, by *free will,* to follow and love God or to reject him. When a person accepts the Lord, *he* is born again in the spirit. From the new birth on, he has to understand some spiritual principles in order to withstand the onslaught of Satan's spirits against the human mind. The way such spirits can even attack believers is when they permit the evil spirits to attack them in this thinking faculty, which has a special affinity toward them.

According to Watchman Nee's biblical interpretation, Christians can open their minds to demons in many ways. The final two ways stressed by the author caught my eye and my breath and gave me knots in my stomach. They are *a blank mind and a passive will.* I nearly screamed when I read:

"Today's so-called scientific hypnotism and religious yoga are in reality founded upon these two principles. Using the argument that certain methods can be beneficial to mankind, those of this class who perform such techniques as focusing one's attention, sitting silently contemplating and meditating are actually employing these devices to reduce their mind to a *blank* condition and their will to passivity so as to invite supernatural spirits or demons to supply them with many wonderful experiences. Our purpose here [in this book] is not to inquire whether or not these people realize they are inviting evil spirits to come, we merely wish to observe that they are fulfilling the requirements for demon possession. The consequences are grave; perhaps later they shall awaken to the fact that what they have welcomed are indeed evil spirits."

My hands shook when I laid the book down for a moment to comprehend what I had just read. "Lord," I said aloud, "Rollie got himself totally involved in yoga and transcendental meditation the summer our home broke up."

I began to recall things in the new light I had just received. Rollie had not only become a different person last spring and summer, he often wouldn't even make sense to the children or me.

He seemed obsessed by frightening wild thoughts, and it was obvious that he couldn't turn off his mind—even at night he would toss and turn for hours.

I remember the night he came home after midnight from one of his meditation sessions with his university friends, who were mostly women. When he got ready to go to bed, an evil presence seemed to walk into the upstairs area with him. I felt so frightened even after I prayed that I took my pillow and cover and fled downstairs. I sat in front of the still-glowing fireplace and watched its light dispel the darkness. I knew that I was up against something dangerous, an evil supernatural threat which puzzled me. I did not know what to do about it except to pray to God to protect us.

As I continued to read Watchman Nee's book, the agonizing puzzle of my whole last year began to form a picture in my mind, and I began to understand. The evil spirits can make a person say and do things which his own heart condemns.

"How many there are who cannot restrain their tongues from gossiping, jesting and backbiting. Their heart is clear, but they are unable to end or restrict these unprofitable words. It seems that as soon as ideas have moved into their mind (brought there by evil spirits) and before there has been any opportunity to think them through, they have already become words. Thoughts rush in in waves compelling the person to speak. The tongue is out of control of the mind and the will. A torrent of words is uttered without thinking or choosing. Sometimes they are spoken against the intent and will of the speaker. Later, reminded by others, they wonder why they have thus spoken."

In my mind, I saw Rollie again sitting across the table at our last anniversary dinner, when I asked him, "*Why* are you saying such horrible things about me? You know me better than that."

And I saw his tortured look when he said, "Something *makes* me say it."

Watchman Nee points out that Jesus can set us free from the control of the evil spirits in our mind. When we ask him for that help, admit that we are controlled by something stronger than ourselves, and resist Satan with our will, in the power of the Holy Spirit (even though our will has been weakened), the Lord will do the rest.

I am not sure that Rollie would listen if I tried to talk to him about it. I am praying that God will use somebody to let him know what he is up against.

I have not a question in my mind that Rollie never realized what he was doing when he got mixed up with that new philosophy. It appealed to his intellectual and complex mind. He has always been very proud of his great intellect, and even after he accepted the Christian faith, he would say ever so often to me, "I can't believe like you do. You are like a child. My mind has to be able to analyze and understand before I can believe."

He never went, in his personal faith, past his own understanding—and he was proud of it.

A week after I had finished the last volume of the three enlightening, helpful volumes of Watchman Nee, I went before the Lord in fasting and prayer. "Show me if there are any evil spirits in me," I prayed. "I understand now that the listlessness, depression, and fear of an unknown threat which have sapped my life these last few weeks are satanic. I am asking for help and shall engage my will as best I know how; just show me what to do."

God showed me last night. "It is time that your *will* forgives everyone who ever hurt you," he said. "Remember, your emotions cannot heal unless your will makes the first step and says, 'I forgive.' "

"I thought I had forgiven where I needed to do so," I said to God.

God took me back to my childhood and scene after scene flashed before my inner eye. Whenever I cringed inside, I knew I hadn't yet been healed. And the wounds couldn't heal because my will hadn't forgiven yet.

Last night I said many times, "I forgive you," loudly into the darkness of my lonely room, to many people in my past. I said it to my harsh foster father, to my foster brother, to enemies and to church saints, and I said it to my husband: "I forgive you, Rollie, I *do* forgive you for everything you do or say. You might not even want to do those things, but you *are* doing them and it hurts. I forgive you!" I sobbed my heart out.

"Now forgive yourself," God said lovingly.

I cried and said it: "I forgive myself, Jesus, because you have forgiven me first."

I wept some more, and every tear I shed seemed to wash the mildew from my soul.

This morning I looked up and the sun was shining.

SEPTEMBER/ *Monday Morning*

One year and a world tour later I am returning to my old diary recordings. As I've read what I wrote just a few short months ago, I can hardly believe that so many things could have happened so fast.

The divorce went through. I will never forget the moment when I walked beside my lawyer into the courtroom. I felt like an actor in a stage play. I couldn't shake the strange conviction that the whole thing was unreal, just another nightmare! It wasn't *I* who stood up when the judge entered. Then I heard *my* name for *my* case.

I had been in courtrooms before as a teacher to plead for some of my troubled students. Once I had followed a judge out when he left; I wanted to convince him to let one of my students graduate. He had sentenced him to a year in prison. The boy was only two months away from his high school graduation. The judge listened attentively when I explained the problem, and he granted my request. He also thanked me for my warm interest toward such troubled youngsters.

It was a different judge who handled my divorce case. He had a tired face and he seemed to be under the pressure of time. He asked me if I wanted extra time for an attempt at reconciliation.

"No, your honor," I said quietly. He granted the uncontested divorce without further delay.

Rollie wasn't there, but one of my neighbors was. She sat in the spectators' section, watching with big curious eyes. Then she came after me when my lawyer and I left.

"Where is your husband?" she demanded, rather disgustedly.

"He does not need to be here since he didn't contest the case," my lawyer answered for me.

The woman looked almost indignant that we had dared to spoil her own thrill and fun for the day. Had she anticipated a Hollywood drama in the courtroom? Did she waste a half-day and miss her favorite TV soap opera in order to stare into my tearless, composed face and hear three or four dispassionate sentences which settled one divorce case among a hundred others?

"Why did you come?" I asked the pushy woman. "I had told you *not* to come, but to pray for us as a family."

She shrugged her shoulders. "The courtroom is open to anyone," she snapped. "I just wanted to see it when *you* got a divorce!"

I walked out. Her eagerness to see something sensational at my expense hurt me more, at that moment, than the fact that my divorce had really become final.

Why must people be so tactless and inconsiderate? I wondered, as Mary drove me from the courtroom to a luncheon. I was scheduled to speak for a club. I did speak and managed to smile and shake hands. Finally it was time to drive back to the mountains by nightfall.

"I forgive you, June," I said aloud into the lone darkness when at last I reached my home, crawled under my blankets, and let the tears roll. "And I am asking you, Lord, to teach her not to be so thoughtless toward others, please. She didn't understand my need for privacy in this hour of humiliation and failure."

Yes, I have learned to say, "I forgive you" many a time since then, to others and to myself, aloud or in my heart. I understand today why God had to lead me through that special August night of last year. I am so glad that he cleansed my soul and showed me that the key to healing is forgiveness. I could never have survived the last months otherwise.

The ministry itself has grown in twelve months. It is really worldwide and has various services. I wouldn't have dared to dream that God would keep Mary and me as busy as we are. We cannot keep up with the demands and the many, many requests to come and speak everywhere. Answering the mail, alone, is a huge task. By now I have spoken all around the world. However, I feel that my main ministry, for the present time, must be in the USA. I love America!

The book about my new life in America is published, too, and selling well. It made the top ten religious bestseller list six weeks after its release.

Another book manuscript about my recent world tour has also gone to the publisher. It is expected to come out before Christmas.

Life for me has become a whirlwind of suitcases, airports, flights, meetings, thousands of faces, and innumerable autographs. I had to learn many new things and I had to learn them fast.

I found out that steady traveling is fun for the first three weeks. Then it becomes very hard work and very tiring. I discovered that a teacher can get sick and stay home, but a speaker cannot. People put too much work and effort into the preparation of my meetings to be let down. Every so often I speak when I really don't feel up to it.

I have learned to shake hands, autograph books, and receive hugs and kisses. I listen to many people after a meeting and never *once* stop smiling, even if I am ready to drop with exhaustion.

If I stop smiling for a moment, I might receive another letter like the one I got from a precious little old lady who wrote to me and said, "Last time I came to your meeting you didn't smile at me as you did the night before. Have I offended you?"

Her letter didn't bother me. I could write back to her and explain that my neck muscles sometimes get so tense from hours of speaking and smiling that I have to "relax" a bit. I also assured her that she was as dear to me as ever before.

Other letters or telephone calls are harder to handle. How is it that I can read 500 letters telling me how people appreciate my messages and how God has spoken to their hearts through my books or my speaking—and the *one* letter which tears me to pieces can wipe out the joy of the other letters for hours or days at a time?

I will never forget the letter that came to our office last fall. It came while I was still hurting badly from a telephone call that Mary had gotten just days before. The call came while I sat in my "hayloft" working on my manuscript. I heard the phone ring downstairs. I knew that Mary was still working in the office, so I didn't need to answer it myself. Something told me to stop writing and go down to find out who had called. It was dusk and no lights had yet been turned on in the house. Mary staggered out of the office before I got there. Her face shone pale white in the semidarkness. She appeared shaken and horrified.

"What happened?" I said alarmed. "Did someone die?"

"No," she said, hardly audible. "Someone from below the mountain called to cancel a meeting she had requested. The girl was very unkind and harsh. I asked her why they canceled you, and she said that your husband has told them everything."

"What is 'everything'?" I asked grimly. Mary tried to ignore the question and talked on.

"Mary," I said firmly, "I want to know *what* was said!"

"Well," Mary finally stuttered, visibly embarrassed, "they know why you got divorced and that you are now living with a woman in the mountains."

I dug my nails into the flesh for a moment. I felt so helpless and angry. "I am so sorry, little Mary," I said. "Your good clean reputation should not be pulled into this. I warned you at the beginning, but somehow I couldn't believe that it would really come to this. After all, Rollie has never even seen or met you. But I should have known better. He seems obsessed with certain ideas."

"It's not me I am worried about," Mary said. "It's you and your work."

We sat down on the stairs and cried. Then we prayed together.

I said it again that night. "I forgive you, Rollie." Next I said: "I forgive you, woman, whoever you are, for being so rash and judgmental against someone you have never met. I forgive you that you have lashed out before you called and *asked us* for an explanation."

A letter came a few days later. It was from a totally different group and seemed to have no connection with the organization which had just canceled. I had been scheduled for a retreat. I was jubilant. Retreats are and always will be my favorite ministry. I am a teacher, and I feel best if I can speak to a group of people more than once. I am aware that true teaching must result in changed behavior for the learner. I never feel that I can teach deeply enough to produce a lasting change through a single meeting. All a simple presentation can do is to whet a listener's appetite, or point to a need.

The letter canceled the retreat. It was a rude letter and ended by saying, "We do not feel that she has *anything* to offer our women."

I had the feeling that someone had taken a knife and stabbed me physically in my heart, I hurt so badly. It took me several days before I could say it again, "I forgive you, whoever you are who wrote the letter. You don't know me. I have never done *anything* to you. I am trying to help other people who hurt when I teach in a retreat. I don't know why you are so cruel, but I forgive you!"

I have taught many retreats since then. At the weekend of the one that was canceled, I was sent by the Lord to speak at a national youth convention. If I like one thing more than retreats, it's to speak to young people. They are my favorite group and I feel most at home with them. They show their love and they come to me with their questions and problems. I love them!

I love GIs, too. I love to talk to them. I think I simply love people! If I can learn to forgive and forget the hurts and remember that people who strike out at me might hurt *more* than I do, God can use me. At least, I hope he can use me a little longer! So many people need to be loved.

Please, Lord, teach me more about love and forgiveness and use me more and more as an instrument of your healing power.

OCTOBER/ *Thursday Morning*

Praise the Lord! I spoke to the group which canceled me by telephone more than a year ago.

It's amazing what God will do when we trust him and

do not defend ourselves. God can work it out, and he did for me! The reason I even mentioned the telephone call to my American dad was because of my concern for Mary. I felt that Mary's reputation was too clean to be dragged down so unfairly. She had lived such a quiet, blameless life always. She had given her heart to Christ when she was nine years old, when a missionary conducted a Vacation Bible School for the children in her town and gave an altar call at the end. Mary stood up, but she was so tiny that the man of God could not see her. He never prayed with her. But God saw the little girl and knew the promise of her young heart. Mary's family were not churchgoers, but she never gave up her decision to follow God. She grew, worked, prayed, waited, and studied hard. She went into church work after her high school years.

I felt that I needed to ask Dr. and Mrs. Walters for advice in this delicate matter. They had been my adopted American parents ever since my full-time ministry began. I had met this precious old couple while visiting Corrie ten Boom in their house. I fell in love with them immediately and trusted them. Dr. Walters had been the president of Corrie's foundation; he also became the first president and leader of our new ministry.

I reported to Mom and Dad the whole incident. I felt terribly confused and needed their wisdom. "Dad," I said, "do I have a *right* to let Mary be dragged into the dirt with me? Wouldn't she be better off to work where she did before?"

I have never seen Dr. Walters angry. He is a very patient and kind gentleman. He didn't show anger then, either. But he turned very quiet and the veins in his temples seemed to become more visible. After a while he said in a quiet voice, "Daughter, neither of you two deserves to be dragged down like that! I shall take care of that matter!"

"But God doesn't want me to defend myself, Dad," I said. "I can only ask about Mary."

"*You* don't need to defend yourself," he said gently, "but God hasn't told *me* that I couldn't stand up and defend *you,* my girl. If I am your father, my name and reputation are here to protect you and Mary." I cried, I was so moved. But I didn't think that anything could really be done.

A few weeks later, we received a letter of apology from the organization—and a request for another speaking appointment. I was overwhelmed. For the first time in my whole life I was experiencing what it meant to have a big strong daddy use his influence and name to protect his child. It gave me a completely new picture of my Father in heaven. Dad's help also gave me new confidence and a deeper love for that grand old man. I am so glad the whole thing happened. Now I know *how* God can bring beauty out of ashes.

It took Mary nearly a year to work out a second date for that group. Right now she is booking engagements for the year after next. I am amazed that people are willing to wait that long for a meeting.

When I finally walked into the chapel of that organization, I spoke to the whole staff. I asked God to help me forget what had happened. "Lord, help me to speak without a chip on my shoulder!" I said in my heart. And God did what I asked for. I forgot the past phone call and let God have his way. He had a message for all those dedicated workers, and the response was genuine and warm. Many thanked me afterward for the special inspiration they had received. They promised to dream bigger dreams for God. I was jubilant. I am convinced that God has put me in a special training school ever since I obeyed him and stepped out into this new ministry.

Two spiritual principles have come very clearly into focus in this past year. First, God and his promises are real and he keeps his Word. He can be trusted. Second, Satan is real, too, and he fights dirty. He is out to destroy and kill at any cost. He uses anything and anybody to attack God's children. He even uses many church mem-

bers and so-called Christians to wound each other's
hearts.

It struck like a needle in my heart when I heard the
statement for the first time: "The evangelical Christians
are the *only* group who shoot their wounded." I groaned
when I began to think about it.

Oh, how I wish that it were not a true saying, but I am
afraid it applies to the daily happenings of many church
communities. I would have never known or believed that
so-called Christians could be so cruel to their fellow believers until I myself came under attack. I am beginning to
understand why God did not permit me to speak about
my broken home in public before this time. If I did,
people would have had to take sides—either for or
against me. And their loyalty should never be for a man
or woman, but to God only. The message I give is either
from God or it is from the devil. Christians can tell *who*
speaks by the fruit of a message. If what I say brings
people to repentance and closer to God, it must be said
through God's Spirit. The devil wouldn't want to lead
anyone to Christ!

So many people tell me that *God* has spoken to them
through my written or spoken words. I always wonder if
they would *still* say it if they knew that I am alone. Would
it then suddenly be not of God anymore?

Sometimes I get so tired and confused about the whole
thing. Friends tell me that I *must* speak up in my defense.
My silence is giving consent to all the accusations, they
say. Others claim I deliberately hide the truth and deceive
the public.

One woman walked up to me and said, "You have no
right to be up in the pulpit. Who do *you* think you are?"

Yes, who am I, Lord? I don't know *why* you told *me* to
go and speak for your cause. I know I am not worthy, but
what can I do but obey and go where you want me to
go?

I said it to the woman who attacked me so righteously.

"You are right," I nodded at her and smiled as if she had given me a kind compliment. "Sister, you are *so* right. I have no business being up here preaching. I know it best! But don't say it to me; tell God off! He is the one who gives me my orders. I have told him a hundred times that he must find somebody better and more worthy than I am, but he just tells me to go. Maybe he can't find anyone *better* who will obey and go. Would *you* be willing to go in my place if God told *you* to give up your home and step out?"

The zealous woman turned on her heel and walked away without a word. I wished she had answered me, for I have no answers myself. I just want to obey God the best I know how. And if I am doing the wrong thing, *he* will have to show me! I'd rather stay home, anyway, and God knows it!

NOVEMBER/ *Wednesday before Thanksgiving*

I never left home with a heavier heart than when I had to leave for my recent tour. Now these seven long weeks of travel have just come to a great end, and I am overflowing with joy and thanksgiving. It surely didn't start out that way, and I feel very ashamed before my Lord. Why can't I ever remember how God has led me in the past? Why must I always fuss, worry, rebel, and act up like a dumb little kid before my heavenly Father? Why can't I simply trust him?

I just didn't want to go on that tour and I told God so. I felt that I had a *right* to stay home. After all, my son Peter needed me. Were not other mothers permitted to look after their children? Why wasn't I?

Peter came to live with me in August before this school year began. He didn't want to stay with his dad anymore.

I learned something the hard way again. One can lead a horse to the well but can't make him drink. I thought I could force Rollie by law to be a father and give Peter the male companionship he needed so badly. The divorce settlement stated that Rollie had custody of our younger son, by my request. I knew that our teenage boy needed a dad more than a mother. He ended up having neither. Rollie is too occupied with his own conflicts to have time for anyone but those who can meet his personal needs. And Peter had a lonely, miserable year. His father was gone most of the time.

When I offered Peter the opportunity of living with me, he showed guarded joy. "Are you *sure* you want me?" he said.

"Of course I do, honey," I said. "After all, I am your mother. The only reason why I didn't keep you last year was because I felt that your dad and you needed each other."

My boy's face turned hard. "I don't want to talk about it," he said, and his hands formed fists. "If I stay with you I don't *ever* want to discuss anything about dad, the divorce, or any of that ugly stuff. I've heard all I want to hear, OK?"

"Agreed," I said. "But I have a few rules to lay down for both of us, too."

I set up some written agreements for Peter and for me, his mother. He agreed not to use pot, alcohol, or nicotine. He would study for decent grades, be in at a certain time on school nights, and not use foul language in our home.

I agreed to spend time with him when not on tour, not to nag or preach, and to trust him.

We both signed the contract and I pinned it over Peter's bed.

The first few weeks I was home with Peter, he carried an invisible wall around himself and nobody seemed to be able to break through. I didn't say much, but prayed a lot. I knew that Peter had gotten the worst of the breakup. It had hit him at his most vulnerable age—as a young teenager. At a time when he was groping with his own changing body and mind, his secure world had broken apart. He was insecure, bewildered, afraid ever to trust again.

I prayed for patience and wisdom. I knew Peter was not keeping the agreements he had signed. Six years of teaching dope addicts and problem students had given me a sixth sense for detecting marijuana smokers by smell and behavior cues. I was sure that Peter was still smoking grass in and out of our home!

What should I do? Kick him out? Ignore it? Talk to him about it? I did none of these. I just stormed my heavenly Father's throne-room with silent prayer for help and wisdom.

The first breakthrough came one Sunday afternoon. Dr. and Mrs. Walters had asked Peter and me to go with them to their church. Dave Wilkerson, the author of the book *The Cross and the Switchblade,* spoke to an overflow crowd.

Peter called my American parents Grandpa and Grandma. He had taken a great liking to them, but stayed guarded. At the meeting, he sat between me and Grandma.

The speaker talked about the need of young people to forgive their erring parents. "There are many in this audience who need to forgive their fathers," Wilkerson said. "Your dad is too busy. He isn't paying attention to you. He is running after money or a more important position. Nevertheless, God said you must *honor* your parents, even if they haven't done right by you."

Then he invited the young people who needed to forgive to come down to the altar to pray a prayer of forgiveness.

I shall never forget what I saw: hundreds of young people walked down every aisle to pray, some crying, some hand in hand with their parents.

My tears had begun to flow before the altar call had been given. I looked up at Peter. His face was as hard as a stone. He shook his head defiantly.

Grandma and I both reached over at the same time to stroke Peter's arms. The preacher began to pray. Suddenly I felt Peter's head on my shoulder and he began to sob. His whole body shook, and I put both arms around him and held him tight.

We cried together, my boy and I. I forgot that he had grown a head taller than I and that he now smoked and cursed God. He was my baby again, and I just held him and felt his hot tears soak through my blouse.

Things got better after that, but he still refused to talk about two issues: God and the divorce.

He struggled in school. He had agreed to go to a Christian high school where the scholastic demands were extremely high. He studied long hours every night. He hated studying—and he hated the school and the teachers. He argued with them, he sassed, he acted up. I knew why: Peter wanted some male attention, but nobody heard the cry beneath his rough behavior. They just scolded and punished him. I pleaded with the principal to give my boy a few minutes of his time. If he or a teacher could just *talk* to him, not only when he needed to be punished, but when he had earned some words of praise and acceptance—but it was to no avail. Everybody seemed too busy to care for a tall, lonely bewildered boy and for his soul. All that seemed to matter were grades.

I watched Peter grow bitter again, and the time for my seven-week departure drew close. I felt desperate, afraid, rebellious. How could I leave Peter alone for seven weeks? One week before I had to leave, he started to have a sore throat.

I prayed for long night hours. "Please, Jesus," I

begged, "make him well. I simply cannot leave him behind when he is not only so confused but also physically ill. Please, Lord, hear my prayers."

Peter got worse. Nothing seemed to help.

The last night, he called me at midnight and asked me to come into his room. He felt hot, and his throat was swollen and covered with blisters.

"Mom," he said hoarsely, "you said Jesus can heal me in an instant. Why doesn't he? You are leaving, and who will take care of me? I am alone in the house. . . ."

"Peter," I said and stroked his feverish head, "I have prayed and prayed for you. God tells me that something stands between you and him which I cannot remove. *You* have to do it. It's *you* who has to pray for healing, not I."

"I cannot." Peter looked tortured and afraid. "I have tried to pray. Every time I try, I see demons rush in on me and they yell and scream and curse. . . ."

I felt chills go down my back. So I was meeting Satan on his old "demon"stration ground again. He wasn't satisfied that he had managed to break up my home; now he was after my child. Peter was God's property. I had dedicated him to God, just as I had my older children. I had given all of them to God and his service soon after they were born. Peter was twice dedicated. I knelt down after he was born—he was premature and wasn't supposed to have lived—and I gave him to God. A year later he almost died of spinal meningitis. The doctors saw no hope for him, but he came back from the hospital completely recovered. It was a miracle, and I knew that God had spared my baby for something special. I told Peter every so often as he grew up that his life belonged to God because he was a living testimony to God's healing powers. Now that power had stopped flowing—or had it?

I looked at Peter. "Do you *want* the demons to leave you? I can tell them to leave, honey, for we Christians have the power over them in Jesus' name."

My son nodded, trembling with fear. "Make them go

quickly, Mommy, they are everywhere. They are moving in. . . ."

I lifted my hand, shaking with anger at the great deceiver, who dared to torture my boy who was God's property. I closed my eyes. "In the name of Jesus," I prayed, "I bind you, Satan. I command you evil spirits and demons to leave my child alone and go away. Father, send the demons to the place you have prepared for them. Make them leave this home and never come back."

"Mom!" Peter touched and interrupted me. "The demons are all gone!" He smiled a happy smile. "I feel fine and so relieved." He jumped out of bed, folded his hands, and said, "Dear Jesus, please come into my heart. Wash my sin away and take my life into your hands."

We talked into the early morning hours. The wall between us had gone. My son had been set free and we communicated again. He finally fell into a refreshing sleep. I left the next morning for seven weeks of a grueling schedule.

Now I am back, and Peter and I have talked again for most of the night. We had to tell each other a lot. We both went through seven weeks of struggles and victories with Christ, and God did such great things for both of us. We cannot thank him enough. We laughed and cried. We prayed together and finally I tucked him in again. Today we are driving north together to be with Kathy and Heidi. We'll all spend the Thanksgiving weekend together at our German friend's house. What a feast it will be!

DECEMBER/ New Year's Eve

What a delightful month this has been—and what an eventful year has gone by!

My American dad rented a cabin in the mountains for

all of us, for four whole weeks. He and his wife are so good to me and my children. They know that we all love the mountains. We have lived at the beach for more than a year now, and it's much more practical and safe. The mountain roads are hard to drive on in fog, ice, and snow, so I finally consented to move down to the ocean before last winter.

God has given us a nice place near the beach, but I don't feel at home unless I can look out the window and see an evergreen tree. For the last four weeks I have been "home" again. The song of the wind in the large fir trees lulled me to sleep every night. Noisy blue jays woke me up every morning. It is amazing how much bird feed they can devour. It's also amazing how much seven young people can eat during one short Christmas vacation.

For the last two weeks Tim, Kathy, Heidi, Peter, and three more young men filled the cabin with noise, laughter, hair curlers, skis, wet socks, cookie crumbs, games, and fireside chats. The fireplace crackled during the cold but sunny days and long into the nights, as we sat around and rediscovered each other as a family.

I can hardly believe that it was only *one* short year ago that I spent Christmas overseas. Was it only such a short time ago that I was a confused, lonely woman who believed she had lost her home and family forever?

Tim lived with his girl friend, and the three younger ones spent last Christmas with a family near their boarding school in the Midwest. Kathy was practically engaged to the son of that home. I was greatly disturbed, but had nothing to say about the matter.

Yes, last year the tensions ran high on both sides. I felt resentful that I was permitted to pay the bills, but had no right to advise or influence. Kathy's future mother-in-law had taken over that position for all three of my younger children.

Kathy returned last spring. She had broken her engagement off and came west to go to school near home.

"Mom," she said, as communication began to flow again, "I resented it that you didn't approve of Donald. I thought he would offer me everything I needed. A quiet farm home, no public attention, a chance to live away from people and city life. . . ."

"Is *that* what you wanted for your whole life?" I asked, surprised. Kathy is more like me than any of the other four children, and her creative personality detested boring routines and a humdrum life ever since she was born.

"I thought I did," Kathy said with her usual honesty. "Because I had rejected you, I tried to become just the opposite of you. But when we began to discuss wedding plans, I got scared. Donald's mother was so hard to please. She ran our lives. *She* told me what I was supposed to be and do for her great son. The final straw came when she said to me, 'Your whole family is trash. . . .' "

I sat and listened and tried hard to keep a straight face. I also fought tears and anger. Why would the woman call us trash before she ever knew all of us?

"Mom," Kathy continued, not even aware in her young self-preoccupation how deeply her words hurt me, "I began to think. Donald's mother calls herself a Christian. She had no right to call our family trash, regardless of what happened."

"Honey, what *did* any one of us do to make us trash?" I asked quietly.

"Well, the divorce and Tim living with a girl, and . . ."

"Do you think Jesus would call us trash?" I said, failing to control my tears any longer.

"No, Mom, and we are not trash." Kathy hugged me. "That's why I decided to call the whole thing off. I suddenly realized that I couldn't just pull all my family roots out and deny or reject my own family, just because some tragedy happened. My first loyalty belongs to *my* family, not to his family. After all, I am part of this family and I do belong. You have never called me trash and you accepted me when I came back. . . ."

Heidi returned to Kathy's college this fall. Both girls are now attending the same school that Tina (and I) graduated from. They are living in the dormitory but come home on vacations.

Tim isn't living with his girl friend anymore. He broke it off. He is now in one of the best known colleges in the state, working toward a science degree. He lives in an apartment. He looked rather tired when he drove in for this Christmas vacation. He has to study day and night.

I am enjoying myself as in olden days. I cook for the gang, listen to their talks, pamper and admonish them, read to them from my new manuscript. We also go for long walks together. I can't believe what all God has been able to restore within *one* year.

I feel loved and accepted, and the children have become rather protective of me. Tim and I have formed a deep bond of mutual respect and friendship. His former girl friend and I are still very close friends, too, though Tim isn't going with her anymore. She calls me every time she gets depressed or lonely. I love her and she knows it. Someday she'll find the source of peace, I am sure.

"You have something I need," she said the other day. "I could accept your brand of Christianity. You don't condemn or treat me like dirt."

Tim said something similar when we had gone on a little walk together, just he and I. "Mom," he said thoughtfully, "I admire you. What you did with your life took courage, a courage I don't have so far.

"I was the one who told you not to resign and give up all your financial securities. Today I have to admit you did what was right for you. You are experiencing something very few people have—the fulfillment of your life's dream. You *are* doing what you want to do *most* and you are happy. I like your type of Christianity."

I looked at him. Was I happy? I hurt inside, very

deeply, but I seldom let it show. I have no right to overshadow my children's lives with my personal loneliness and failed womanhood.

I wasn't sure I was as happy as he thought I was, but I do carry a deep joy in me at all times: God's gift of joy.

Happiness is like a bright, murmuring brook that dances and sings in the sunshine and runs down the mountain as long as circumstances are fine. When the drought and storms come, the waters dry up. Dirt and rocks can plug up the spring.

Joy, as God gives it to his children, is like a deep well, and the water never dries up. Sunshine or rain, storm or thunder, the well stays full, for joy does not depend on happy circumstances, but on God.

I knew that I could put my trust in God, but little did I know what a considerate "Abba" my heavenly Father would be.

Here we are, my children and I. We had the biggest Christmas ever. (Grandma saw to that.) We had gifts heaped high under the tree, more food and goodies than we could eat, fun and laughter, a stay in a lovely mountain cabin, friends who come and go—we live like royalty!

Heidi said it while she sat in front of the blazing fireplace sketching Tim's head, the rest of us watching her while listening to soft Christmas music: "Aren't we lucky? We live like the rich people."

I winked at Tim. "Why shouldn't we?" I said, and joy welled up in me so deeply that I couldn't keep my tears back. "After all, your mother works for the King of the Universe—and he *is* the best paymaster!"

Tomorrow the children will leave to be with their father; then they must go back to school.

I have three children in college and one in a private Christian high school. I am glad that my Father in heaven owns all the silver and gold and the cattle on a thousand hills.

It takes that kind of a provider to handle the needs of this family. But God has done *more* than I dared to dream or ask for. How can I ever thank him enough?

JANUARY/ *Saturday Morning*

My staff enjoyed the cabin, too. They came up several times. Mary and I were not able to do all the work by ourselves any longer, so God sent us help during the last year. I now have a growing office family, too.

Cheri is our new office manager. Tricia works in shipping and mailing. Elisabeth is my consultant and has become a very special friend of mine. She has not joined our group yet, but she will someday. I believe God desires it. I wonder how long it will take before we can hire her. It seems almost impossible that she ever would give up her present position as a senior executive in one of the leading evangelical organizations.

Well, I don't worry about it! God has done so many impossible things for this young ministry; he will bring about what is his will in his own good time.

Elisabeth and Mary came up New Year's Day to share my last day in the cabin. What a peaceful, quiet, and beautiful day we had! First, fog wrapped itself around the little house like a protective blanket and muffled every sound. Even the blue jays seemed to sleep in. Then gentle but thick snow began to fall, covering the earth with the promise of a new spring. The mountains were so parched by last year's drought that I stood at the window and cried with joy and gratitude to God for the life-giving moisture. My friends, the trees, needed water so badly! Snow would help them more than rain. Warm rain would run off fast and not seep into the hardened ground as much as the slow-melting snow could next spring.

What symbols God provides in nature for his children, if we really look and listen. How often we stand before

God and complain because we don't understand what he
is doing. How often I have said to God in the last year:
"Lord, I feel cold and lonely! Why can't you send me
into a warm and gentle spring rain of new, deep human
relationships? Why must I be so alone? I know I have you
at all times, but sometimes I long for the expression of
your love through another close human friendship."

For the last few years all the life-giving moisture to my
soul has come in the form of snow. I had no close personal warm relationships—no complete opening of the
heart to anyone but God.

God is a Spirit, and the only way we can commune
with him is through our spirits. My spirit had communion,
but my human soul, especially my emotions, dried out.

In the last few months the snow in my soul started to
melt. I am beginning to form new, deep friendships. I
dare to open myself again.

I wonder if anyone who has gone through an experience like mine has had the problems I struggled with? I
did have a hard time trusting anyone beyond a certain
point, ever since I felt betrayed by Rollie. Sure, I have
had many friends—hundreds of them—and all over the
world. We share friendly fellowship in the Lord and I am
grateful for them. But they don't know the depth of my
soul and neither do I know them in this way.

Elisabeth is the first person I have begun to open myself up to. I let her see the dry ground of my parched soul
and I dare to be myself around her: happy, depressed,
rejoicing, searching, afraid to trust, ever-so-human.

She is my elder, but not old enough to be a mother,
rather a mature friend. She is my superior in many as-
pects: she is a specialist when it comes to media, ancient
Jewish culture, Old Testament literature, Bible knowledge,
the present story of Israel, and many other areas I know
very little about. But we seem to think alike. And I am
learning much as we share and listen.

The first three weeks of last month I wrote a Bible

study for babes in Christ. I have sensed the need for it in every audience I have ever spoken to. I always make an appeal for people to invite Christ into their hearts. Every so often someone would come up afterward and say, "I did it. I invited Jesus into my life. Now where do I go from here?" I couldn't find any literature that suited me to give to that newborn babe in Christ. So God told me to sit down and write that baby-book—without denominational slant, without clichés, without complex theology —just plain milk of the Word.

I could never have done it without the help of Elisabeth. She spent long hours and days advising, editing, writing a study guide to go with the book—and never accepting a penny of pay for all of her hard work. Her complete devotion to God and her unselfish willingness to help without any thought of repayment or recognition warmed my heart.

We talked most of New Year's Day about God's plans for the future of our ministry. She believes that God will make it a worldwide teaching ministry. It scares me to think that we could grow much bigger. I don't have what it takes now to head up the growing organization. I remind the Lord every so often that I am only a little orphan girl from the hayloft and know not which way to go. I feel like Solomon: I am but a little child!

God assures me over and over that he knows what he is doing and that I can trust him in everything. He will send me people to help when I need them most. And Elisabeth will someday take some of the burdens from my shoulders—when God's time has come.

We went for a walk before she helped me pack the car and clean the cabin. Mary had already left. I told Elisabeth what God had shown me.

"I am ready whenever God is," she said simply.

I am so grateful to God for that last quiet reassuring day in the mountains. The sun had come out after the heavy snowfall ended. I stood and soaked in the almost unearthly beauty of my beloved winter wonderland. Pure white snow and golden sunlight on the mountains, symbols of God's forgiving love and power. What rich splendor! What glory! What deep assurance for me!

I am closing my eyes every so often and recalling these moments as life gets tough again—and it has been ever since I came down the mountain.

I left the day after New Year's to fly with Mary by private plane to Mexico. I had been asked to investigate a certain disaster area in Baja and see if an orphanage could be started by an American missionary who had worked there for many years. He needed help and his organization called on us. It is known by now that I have a soft spot in my heart and room in my budget for orphans.

I came back, raw in my intestines and my soul. A dam had broken and swept thousands of people into the bay. The people who survived had no homes or beds left, no food, no sanitation, no clean water.

Many children wandered around, orphaned, uncared for, living on handouts and refuse. Hundreds of families lived in tents sent by American organizations, or in shelters built from boxes or cartons.

I looked at the indescribable human misery and wondered if my own world was a dream, a beautiful fairy-tale dream. Was it really I who just had spent four glorious weeks in a warm, clean, comfortable mountain cabin with plenty of food, sleeping on rose-printed sheets on a canopy bed, surrounded by four happy, healthy children and many friends? Had the sun really shone upon glistening snow in a world of affluence, freedom, peace, and order? Was my world truly only three flight hours to the north, away from such bleak and ugly human struggle for survival?

I was sick when I got home. My diarrhea stopped after one day, but the pain in my heart is still deep.

I pray that I shall never complain again. While we in

America gripe about petty little inconveniences, the world around us is dying in hardship and agony.

What I can do to relieve human suffering, I will do. If I had no other reason (and I do since I know Christ's commission), I would want to help because I am permitted to live in America. The rest of the world would love to be here! I shall never know why I am so blessed and privileged.

May I never take my blessings and privileges for granted again!

FEBRUARY/ *Wednesday Night*

I almost went alone on my speaking tour to the Midwest and the East Coast of the U.S.A. Mary ended up in the hospital for several days after we returned from Mexico. The English language has several names for the bug which attacks the intestines of innocent American travelers in the land of the Aztecs. "Montezuma's revenge" is one of them. Whatever one calls it, it's a radical way to lose weight! I had only a slight touch of it, but Mary suffered severe dehydration. I wonder how we got it? We were so careful not to drink any unboiled water. Mary did have two ice cubes in a soft drink because she was too polite to refuse them. We were in one of the best Mexican hotels of the city and she had felt safe.

Traveling can be hazardous, and Satan has tried his best to make life hard, inside and outside of the country.

Well, Mary survived, and, though weak and looking pale, she was able to accompany me into the most severe winter weather we have experienced for many years.

We couldn't get warmed up for days. What a horrible winter the Midwest and East had! At the same time the West had not a drop of rain, only unreasonable summer heat. But if I ever doubted whether God was completely in control of everything, I saw it on this tour.

In spite of blizzards, storms, and icy roads, every meeting we were scheduled for took place, and the meeting halls ended up overcrowded. People did a lot of praying in our behalf, and God answered in the most visible ways.

I shall never forget places like Fort Wayne, Indiana. I had spoken there several times before, but this last time God's working was clearly revealed to many of the people present, not only to us.

Last year we almost got caught in a hotel fire in that city. It killed one woman and injured twenty-three other hotel guests. Mary and I were not in it because we missed a plane. If the devil tried to make it hot for us on that previous trip, this time we ended up freezing!

The snowstorm was supposed to hit the day I had to speak for a citywide prayer breakfast. How the people prayed for a delay—and God did what we asked for. He delayed the blizzard until the meeting was over. The people got safely home, and we were on our way to the airport by the next afternoon.

Somehow we all overlooked asking God to hold the howling winds until our plane had taken off. By the time we fought our way into the air terminal, the runways had closed because of high snowdrifts. But the airport finally reopened, and we then spent seventeen sleepless hours in various airports between flights trying to make it in time in order to keep our next appointment in Jackson, Mississippi.

There the same thing repeated itself. A snowstorm was predicted for the Sunday afternoon I had been scheduled to speak in one of Jackson's largest churches. A group of young couples who had attended one of my retreat meetings the day before had special prayer in their Sunday school. They asked God to hold the snow until the meeting was over. And God did it again. The church was packed with people. After the meeting we walked out into the first gentle snowfall. The audience hurried home, for

southern cities are practically paralyzed when they get
frost or snow. They have no snowplows, no salt, nothing
to make the streets passable. It took some very careful
driving for my friend Monica to get us to the airport the
following morning.

What a way to live! I wouldn't do it for anything or
anybody but for my Lord!

I often get amused when some starry-eyed youth asks
me, "How does it feel to be a famous author and to
travel all over the world speaking?"

One bored, precious housewife came up to me after a
meeting and said, "I envy your life-style. I would give
anything if I could travel like you do!"

I looked at her and said with a smile, "That's exactly
what it takes to do what I am doing—you have to give
anything: your comfort, your own bed, your leisure, your
right to go to bed when you feel sick, your private life,
your enjoyment in being with those you love. . . ."

I was careful not to tell her that there were even more
deprivations than that: delayed airplanes, bad weather,
poor restaurant food with danger of food poisoning and
other inconveniences of travel. All these can become a
way of life, and I have learned to accept them.

But things begin to get to me when I have to face raw
hate from people I don't even know. In the last year I
have had several death threats.

One such telephone call woke us up after midnight. It
was last spring, just after I had finished some meetings in
Colorado. Mary answered, listened, slammed down the
receiver, and then called the front desk. She requested
that we be moved immediately to a "safer" room. Someone had decided that I needed to be killed. What a night
that was! I had a hard time convincing the hotel au-
thorities that I didn't want the police to come.

I didn't want a police escort to go to the airport the
next morning, either. We changed our flight time and the
airline and flew out under other names. I believe that one

should be careful under such circumstances and not act foolishly. But I can't see *how* police could stop someone from shooting at me if the person is determined to do so.

I have a deep conviction that God is *all* the protection I need. However, I must admit that I am not a fearless superwoman. My heart and head know that I don't need to be afraid, but my stomach and knees feel weak and shaky every time. So I always have to make a decision: Do I act according to my will or do I let the butterflies in my stomach control me? I know better than to act on my feelings, ever, but my human weakness can do some strange things to my head. So I "act" courageously and say the "right" things, as a Christian should. I pray and ask God to take care of me—and then I begin to protect myself. How? By looking into people's faces and wondering if anyone is following me. . . .

I studied faces while we flew from Colorado to Texas. When we arrived at my next stop, we found out that some "friends" had already called and asked when I would arrive, and when and where I would speak. My butterflies had a wild time again.

When I walked up to the pulpit for a double Sunday morning service, I asked God to help me forget any threats and speak his words only. During the preliminaries I studied faces again. I wondered what a person who might shoot me would look like. I tried to shake my fearful guessing and stood up to speak. Slowly the strain left—until I saw a tall man walking in the foyer. He walked up and down, up and down, and never entered the sanctuary. I looked at him. He was middle-aged, tall, handsome, and dark—he looked like a typical Hollywood gangster figure. Suddenly I began breaking out into a cold sweat. I felt myself drowning in fear and my mind went blank.

"Jesus," I called in my heart, "help me!"

The fear left, my thoughts began to form orderly words, and I finished the message.

The same man marched up and down in the second service, and I became convinced that he had sinister intentions. Once in a while he looked toward me as I spoke. I became numb inside. After the service, I walked to the main exit to shake people's hands. The man stayed close and watched me. When the crowds thinned, he finally stepped toward me. I held my breath and my heart skipped a beat.

He stretched out his hand and said, "I appreciated your messages so deeply. I am one of the elders of this church, and I apologize for not coming in." He lowered his voice. "The minister asked me to stay out here and watch, since we seemed to have a security problem. We also had a sheriff here in plain clothing. He is an elder, too, and we know our people. So we kept an eye on strangers and seated them toward the rear where we could watch them. We stayed for both services."

I almost hugged the gentleman, but I managed to control myself. He will never know why I had tears in my eyes when I shook his big strong hand. I smiled and thanked him kindly while I conversed with God in my heart at the same time.

"Forgive me, Jesus," I said and giggled to myself, "and I thank you for your precious way of teaching me to trust you! God, you have a perfect sense of humor, besides being perfect love and understanding. I am so sorry for acting so dumb. Please have patience with me, and teach me to trust you more fully."

Slowly I am learning to trust Jesus with everything I have, even my nervous stomach and shaky knees.

The last death threat I had was only a few short months ago. It looked like a very sticky situation, and the minister had summoned the sheriff and many plainclothesmen to cover the place.

Mary had called several prayer groups and telephone prayer chains in different parts of the country. Several people had called us back with a special message from

God. *"Nothing* will happen," they said, giving us various Scripture verses as God's pledge. God had given me the same message.

"Go and speak," he said. "No man can touch you!"

I didn't search faces that night. I decided to trust Jesus all the way. The sheriff sat beside me, obviously on pins and needles. Before I got up to speak I turned to him. "Sir," I said and smiled, "don't worry anymore, nothing will happen. You see, I have my *own* secret service."

"You do?" He sounded surprised.

"Yes, I do." I smiled big. "Angels!"

His face fell. "Oh," he mumbled and sat up straight again, to scare the audience.

I finished speaking, and police escorted me to the hotel. They kept the place under observation until we left town. Nothing happened, of course, but I pray ever so much that the message I gave that night may have touched the sheriff and some of the other men who came to protect me.

If only one of them would someday accept Jesus because good seed was dropped into their hearts that evening, it was worth it all.

God has said that the wrath of men shall praise him. And *all* things work together for good to those who love him and are called according to his purpose. I believe it!

MARCH/ *Friday Night*

God has a way of nudging me gently toward tasks I am not very eager to do!

I spoke to several retreats lately and always managed to get through without saying *anything* about my family. It's an unwritten law and silent agreement I have with my kids that our private life stays out of the public eye as much as possible. Neither my children nor I say much when people try to pry into our family life.

When people ask me how my family is, I say, "Thank you, fine." When they ask me what Rollie is doing, I say, "He is going to school and he works."

One woman came up during a reception and shouted, "Is it true that you left your husband and he is now preparing for the ministry?"

I said quickly, "No, it is not true." And I walked away. I couldn't have said more if I had tried. I simply can't talk about it yet, and people can be so nosy and thoughtless. Why do people think that a public speaker or writer owes it to anyone to disclose anything and everything about his private life?

I was in no way prepared for what happened when I arrived at a women's retreat in one of the central states. The program stated that I was to give a workshop with the topic, "The Black Sheep."

Nobody had asked or forewarned me of the topic. Mary knew nothing about it either. I had been prepared to give my usual retreat messages. I panicked!

"Lord," I prayed, "what do you want me to do about it?"

"Speak as I show you," he said gently. "Just open your heart to the women."

I expected a small workshop group. Instead, the large room was packed with hundreds of women. It did not make my task easier.

"Ladies," I began, "what I am sharing with you this morning is neither in a book nor on any tape of mine. And I prefer it that way. I am asking you to turn off your tape recorders for this message. It is for the time of the workshop and your ears alone. I gave a promise to all my children to protect their privacy, but God has told me to share with you this morning as I have never shared before."

The room was so still, one could have heard a pin drop. Then I began my confession of a mother's confusion and failure. I started by telling that I was an expert on black sheep, for I had been one all my life. "In the English language people have a choice," I said. "They can call problem children either black sheep or creative children." The women relaxed and laughed.

Next I shared how I arrived in America with two model children. My Tina and Tim behaved perfectly and I thought that I could never have a problem child. I simply wouldn't permit it! It was nothing but a matter of strict discipline, I thought.

I had *all* the answers to child-raising for the first six years we lived in America. By then three more children had come to join us, and from their births on I could notice a difference between their behavior and that of my two oldest children.

"It's almost as though something is in the air here in America that encourages children to act up," I said. The women laughed again.

Nevertheless, I still felt completely in control with all five children, until my oldest girl became a teenager.

I had never heard that word before and didn't know what I was in for. My daughter began to reason with me. "Mother," she would say, "I don't think it is of the devil to wear nylons and high heels."

"It *is* of the devil," I would cut her off. "And white socks and oxford shoes are healthier for you!"

"Mom," she would say again another day, "other girls use some mascara and their mothers permit it."

"I don't permit it," I would snap at her. "This is nothing but vanity and the pride of life."

I figured that my answers had convinced my child and settled the argument. They hadn't! Instead they just encouraged my daughter to live with a double standard. She learned to wash the mascara off before coming home from school, and to do other things "behind my back." I never suspected anything.

When Tim hit his teenage years more than three years later, I still hadn't learned much. I thought I was still the "perfect" mother who had everything under control. I got my lessons back this time with greater force. My "model" son exploded in my smug face; I watched an obedient, gentle, intelligent boy become a rebel overnight.

He seemed to make it a point to outsmart me, outtalk me, and convince himself and my younger children that I was a crazy, old-fashioned woman who needed to go to a mental hospital.

"Mother," he would growl in his changing voice, "this is America, OK? Things are different here than they were in *your* land." He sounded as if I had come from the moon. My three smaller children listened and learned.

The battles we fought while he grew toward high school graduation and adulthood are too numerous and painful to mention.

I had gone back to college during that time and fought many other battles, but none were more painful than Tim's change of attitude.

Many sleepless, tearful nights I spent praying, pleading and agonizing before God. "Please, Lord," I would beg, "show me where I failed. I tried so hard to do my best with the children. I had family worship every day. The only music I played in the house was religious records. I took them faithfully to church. I taught them many songs and Bible verses. I did not permit them to live like the world. O God, teach me at any cost. I have three more children growing up, and I can't handle it if every one of them follows the same rebellious ways."

God *will* teach us if we are willing to learn, I found out. I learned slowly, painfully, and the hard way as usual!

I shared with my sisters in Christ that morning in a few minutes what God had shown me through long hard years. My greatest mistake was that I didn't give my children their right to have freedom of choice.

Oh, that struggle with the concept of freedom had been with me ever since I had come to America. As my children grew up I had to face it again! God had taught me through the years the meaning and source of freedom. He himself had given it at the beginning of time to every creature he had made. For love cannot be served and worshiped by force, but by freedom only.

Jesus even died to give the human race its freedom back. Through him men may make a free will choice for or against God again. For Satan had taken the whole human race captive.

Next to the gift of Calvary, freedom of choice is God's greatest gift to mankind. Nobody can touch it without displeasing God!

"You have tried to brainwash your children," God said to me one night. "Someone brainwashed you as a teenager and now you try to do the same."

"But, Lord," I argued back, "I tried to teach them the *right* way. I was taught a lie."

"It is *never* right to *force* anyone, even to make them go my ways," God said to me.

"Don't I have to have rules in the home?" I asked. "I can't permit my children to do as they please. They don't understand what they are doing."

God showed me that I had to make a difference between setting up rules and forcing my children to *think* after me. Rules are needed and should be consistently enforced in the home, but nobody has a right to think for another person. Teenagers already have their own maturing/reasoning power and are capable of conceptual thinking. I finally began to understand that God gave good rules to point us humans to a fulfilled life, but he never forces us to keep his principles. If we break the laws of a godly life, we have to live with the consequences of our behavior. But even then God never lets us down. He just stands gently and lovingly by and helps us carry our self-made crosses. He will not *force* us to be good!

I learned *ever* so slowly, but surely. For my two oldest children my new insights came too late; the damage was done.

Tina had turned very bitter against a Puritan God whom she saw as revengeful, spoiling any fun, and out to punish her for any mistake.

Tim went further than that when I put before him the choice to either abide by the rules of our home or leave. He left! He moved into a house with some friends. They believed in dope, alcohol, free sex, and the "new morality."

I did not know if I would see my Tim's face again.

"I hate you!" he said when he left.

When he came home one afternoon a few months later, just for a visit, God had prepared my heart for it. I didn't preach. I didn't yell. I didn't nag. I simply welcomed him and listened thoughtfully. I told him I was glad to see him. I meant it.

When he got over the shock of suddenly finding a mother who didn't try to make him "be good," he and I began to communicate again. Over a period of time we became friends and discovered fun things we had in common. As I showed my respect and gave him credit that he was thinking for himself, the frequency of his visits increased.

When he chose to go to junior college instead of the expensive private college the family had chosen for him, I told him that I was proud of him and every good grade he made. I saw so many good things in him that I could appreciate.

"Well, by now he is in a special college," I told the women. "He has chosen the school and he studies hard to be what he wants to be: a scientist."

It's a far cry from the dream that I had for him. I raised him to be a missionary doctor.

"Is it fair that we parents try to force *our* dreams on our children?" I asked the women.

Tim has given me great insight into the thinking of our young people. "Look, Mom," he said, "my generation has a different outlook toward the future than you had when you were my age. We look toward adulthood and see the mushroom cloud of an atomic war in the distance."

Another time he said, "Mom, I tried to please you, but I never could come up to your demands; your standards were unreachable."

I told him one day, through tears, how sorry I was that I had made so many mistakes, and I asked him to forgive me because I had tried to manipulate him and force him toward my religion.

He said kindly, "Look, Mom, don't torture yourself anymore. You did what you thought was best at that time. Have you forgotten what the Bible says, 'Train up a child in the way he should go; and when he is old, he will not depart from it'?" He smiled at me. "Give me time, Mother. I am not old yet."

I finished the workshop by telling the women some of the principles I try to follow for my three younger children at the present.

I face the fact that the seed-sowing is *finished* by the age of twelve. I don't nag or preach constantly to the teenagers. They know what I am thinking. They have heard me for many years.

If I feel I need to talk to my maturing children about God, I go *first* to talk to God about my children. He will give me wisdom when to talk and when to be silent. I try to *live* my convictions. I try to be consistent in my sensible rules and save my thunder for the important moral issues, not the often outdated, little cultural pet peeves my Puritan thinking has created. I remember that parents cannot save their children. Since God has no grandchildren, they have to make their *own* decisions to invite Jesus into their lives and become children of the heavenly Father.

Someone asked, "Is there *nothing* that we can do to aid our troubled teenagers?"

"Oh, I believe there is something!" I answered. "We must respect them. The more intelligent children are, the more rebellion can be expected when we try to think for them. They resent it when we don't give them credit that they can think for themselves. We must make an effort to praise them for anything they try to do right, even if they do it differently than we would. We can praise God that he will do what we cannot do: save our children!"

"How can God promise in Isaiah 49:25 that he *will* save our children? Is he not violating his own gift of freedom of choice by it?" another mother asked.

"No, I don't believe so," I said. "Though God will never force anyone against his will to be saved, he *will* hear the prayers of faithful parents (even if they made mistakes) and go after their children."

I am convinced that most of our children are not in Satan's camp completely by free choice. They got trapped into addiction, bad habits, and sin by their youthful curiosity, peer pressure, and our wrong representation of God to them.

First, they enjoy it in Satan's world, for there *is* pleasure in sin for a season. It's when the season of fun is over that they need our love and open arms and reassurance. God is always waiting for them and so can we! Christ will set them free. We don't need to. We need to trust our heavenly Father and accept our children for what they are and where they are. We can pray for them without ceasing.

We cannot force anyone into God's kingdom, but we can love people in, including our children. Praise the Lord for his promises!

APRIL/ *Monday Morning*

The mail we received after the "black sheep" workshop was staggering. I knew that God had done something special that morning. The reaction of the audience said so. In my closing prayer I had asked God to go after our wandering sheep in the wilderness of sin, to bring beauty out of our ashes, and I thanked him for his promise to us erring parents. Most of the women wept; some sobbed when I left the room, crying myself.

Only days later the mail began to pour in. Letter after letter thanked me for the workshop message, for my honesty, for my willingness to share, and for the new hope the morning had brought to many hearts.

One woman wrote that she went home healed! She had previously received shock treatments because she couldn't handle the guilt and worry about her children anymore.

Another woman said: "I can raise my head again. I felt like a total failure when my son left the church, and I took the whole blame. Now I know that he did it by his own freedom of choice. I also know that God can turn my mistakes into something special for my son's life."

One woman wrote: "If *you* have problems with your children, who am I to complain? I never thought that someone like you, who was chosen by God to speak for him, would have the same problems we have in our common Christian homes."

I laid my head on the big pile of letters and wept. "Friend," I thought, "if you only knew! I do not only have the *same* problems, I have more problems than the average. Satan seems to come in like a flood and I hold on to Jesus like sinking Peter!"

I have to remember so often what my friend Lynn said to me shortly after we met. She is a nationally known speaker for God, and we felt drawn to each other from the first moment we met. We both felt the Holy Spirit's prompting to share our personal burdens with each other. She had shared with me about something which nearly destroyed her ministry. It was such a traumatic family crisis.

"I told the Lord I'll never speak again," she said, "and

I meant it. I didn't feel worthy anymore; I had failed him."

She not only spoke for God again, but her words were suddenly filled with a new power of compassion which reached the hearts of many. I knew it because I had heard her and witnessed the healing power of the Holy Spirit in her message for my own life.

She said something to me which has rung in my soul ever since. "Special service for God does not protect us from suffering and agony," she said. "Someone said to me that if Satan cannot attack God's anointed servant himself, he will attack what is *most dear* to that child of God."

How true that is in my life. Nothing could be more important to me than my children—and the devil knows it! He operates in the same way in many other homes. The letters showed me something I wasn't aware of: the Christian home is attacked by *every* evil power under heaven and the religious communities are not willing to admit it.

Many women wrote that they had *never* heard anyone, before that black sheep workshop, speak so honestly on such a subject.

I had to agree. I wouldn't have talked about it either if God hadn't nudged me into it, in spite of my personal reluctance. What makes us Christian speakers so hesitant about being honest behind the pulpit? Why are most messages a report of total victories, a fairy-tale story with a happy ending?

The Bible surely does not give us such a picture. It gives us the honest report of fallible humanity, raw sin, and much error. It also has the answer to man's mistakes and needs: the perfect, unconditional saving power of the love of God. Yes, we are told about justice and God's judgment day, too. But God is first of all Love, and he is eager to bring *every* good thing about *if we let him.*

Oh, the phoniness of our Christian witness! Tolstoy (a famous Russian writer of the past century) said that any worthwhile writing has to be written with the writer's own heart blood or it is not worth being written. That goes for speaking, too—especially if one speaks for God. God wrote the Bible with his own heart blood. Christ, the eternal Word of God, spoke with his own shed blood. Who are we that we should only talk about the pleasant things of Christianity, or of what *we* did *right?*

I shall never forget the time I sat in a retreat shortly after my world had broken apart. I was scheduled to speak along with a well-known Christian lady who lectured on the Christian home. I attended her lecture. She told about some difficulties she and her spouse had faced. She had a foolproof answer: When she obeyed God and submitted herself to her husband, things worked out and God blessed her marriage again.

I sat there and wondered if I was the only one who felt like crawling under the chair. I was devastated, crushed, confused, and I questioned God. Why had he saved her house and not mine? I sat there fighting tears and asking God that question.

"Because it takes *two* to make it work," God answered me. "Her husband wanted to submit and obey, too. And when both sides are willing to do *my* will, then *any* marriage can be saved!"

"Do you want me to point it out to the speaker?" I asked God. I felt humiliated and dejected.

"No, my child," God said gently, "let me show it to her when she is ready for it."

That I wasn't alone when I felt let down and so discouraged by that message was evident by something which happened right after the speaker finished. A young minister's wife came to me and asked me if she could speak to me in private. We found a quiet place and she broke into tears. Finally she controlled herself enough to talk. "I don't know why I am coming to you," she said, "but I felt after prayer that you would understand. You see, I tried what the speaker said. I submitted and obeyed and tried to please my husband the best I knew how. But he is having an affair with the church organist anyway, and he comes and goes as he pleases. He says it's *all* my fault, and I have to go along with it and submit. The Bible says so. I don't know how much longer I can go on. I feel that I am heading for a nervous breakdown."

I looked at her. Her hands shook like leaves. She was thin and pale and obviously an emotional wreck. In my heart, I begged the Lord for wisdom. I felt in no way qualified to give advice. I was too confused on the subject myself. I prayed silently, and assurance and guidance came.

"Honey," I said, "the Bible can be interpreted for any purpose or to prove anything. But it is not true that *one* person must take *all* the blame for a marriage crisis. We are too human ever to be *all* innocent or *all* guilty. However, whatever one does in the end, each one must be responsible for his or her *own* action. We all are gifted by God with our individual personal freedom of choice, and *we* decide our own life and destiny. Your husband chose adultery; you didn't. By that choice and by Christ's words, you are therefore *free* and not obligated to submit to his way of sin any longer.

"As a *free* woman you must go to God and ask him what is best for all of you. The shape you are in, you will crack up unless something gives. If you have children, they deserve at least *one* parent. If your husband is involved with another woman and you are in a mental institution, who has won? Satan!

"As long as your husband chooses sin and does not repent, he has put himself on the side of the unbelievers and sinners. You as a free, Christian woman will have to understand that God does not want his children to be yoked with an unbeliever. Tell your husband that he must make a decision: either he makes things right with God and you, or he leaves to be with the woman. You are not obligated to wash his shirts and take care of him so that he has the time and energy to go to another woman."

"What about the second mile we ought to go as Christians?" she asked.

"Christ told us to walk the *second mile,* not miles without end! I always cringe when I watch Christians playing the role of a doormat in the name of Christ," I answered. "It is a well-known and a valid psychological fact that people resent those who let them get away with murder. Our children and teenagers feel much more secure if we parents set sensible rules and clearly defined limits. They'll try to test us, but they mature better if they know how far they can go.

"In a marriage it is similar. A mate who does what he knows to be wrong by God's standards resents it when he is allowed to do it without objection. If women only knew how much more their husbands would respect them if they acted as equally responsible helpmates, not as brainless, weak sex objects. I have *never* seen it work out right when we Christians condone sin in any form. We must love sinners, but permit them to learn by the consequences of their wrong choices."

I took a deep breath. "At least, that's what God has shown me about my own situation. I filed for divorce, and I believe I obeyed God when I did it."

The woman stared at me with deep shock in her eyes. "*You* are going through a divorce? God help us!" She began to cry. "If you can go through with it and minister to others at the same time, so can I! God has tried to show me what you said through my parents, through the counsel of close friends, but I didn't want to accept it. I thought that if I hang on long enough, things will work out."

We cried and prayed together.

Since then I have long begun to wonder if the Christian community not only has many of their children wandering

as lost sheep in the wilderness, but how many homes are
on the rocks like Elaine's. She and I have been correspond-
ing for almost two years now, and I watch her slowly
putting the pieces of her shattered life back together. Her
husband left, came back, and left again. She finally drew
the line. Since then, her self-respect and human dignity
are being restored by Jesus Christ, who is now her only
Husband and the loving Provider and Father to her three
little children.

I am getting more and more mail from forsaken and divorced people. There seems to be great confusion and
much theological controversy on that issue. Many people
know by now that I am alone. Some of them write for
advice, help, and spiritual guidance. I feel no calling to
split hairs over certain Bible texts, and I avoid taking
theological sides. I just try to point the rejected and lonely
to Jesus. He not only forgives, he heals, restores and
gives new direction to shattered lives. Nobody can argue
with me about that point. I *know* and can testify to that
fact. I pray that God will show me in his own good time
what the Bible really has to say about the whole issue.
Nobody seems to know for sure!

MAY/ *Sunday Evening*

We finally put the Black Sheep message on a cassette
tape. I had Tim's permission to do so. I simply told him
what had happened at the workshop and what response
we had had.

"Mother," my son said, "if our story helps anybody, I'll
be honored if you tell it!"

We recorded it at another retreat, and the reaction to
the message was the same as the first time. I watched
most of the audience fall apart, and nearly everybody
wept.

The new tape is selling by the hundreds and proves

what I have suspected since I gave that message for the first time. There is hardly a Christian home which does not have a problem with at least one or more of its children as they grow up. I find it is almost as though God breaks a dam in the hearts of many sorrowing, silenced parents when they hear my message. Now they write to me, call me, talk to me after meetings, and are so grateful that someone finally dared to talk about it.

I think that a person often feels that he or she *alone* goes through a particular trial; even a family unit might feel that way. It is a great relief to find out that others are in the same boat. Parents who have gone through similar heartaches can understand, comfort, and help each other—if they are open and honest and willing to communicate. And that's where I see the Christian community fail. We are not sharing both sides in our fellowship; we're only reporting the victories, and those mostly to glorify ourselves! Forgive us, God!

One mother wrote, "I sit in church and don't dare to cry. My heart is so heavy, for my children are grown and don't go to church anymore. I cannot talk to anyone, not even to my pastor. I carry so much guilt. Your tape is the first ray of hope in my despair."

How I long to comfort people like her! How I also long to have answers to the many questions about divorce and remarriage that come more and more my way.

Right now for the first time I have an opportunity to meditate on, study, and research that sensitive subject. The Lord has given me most of this month for a beautiful rest. It didn't start that way. Elisabeth and I were supposed to lead a travel group of forty-five people to Israel and Europe. I love Israel and the Jewish people, and I looked forward to the breathtaking beauty of the Alps. But I was so exhausted at the beginning of the month I couldn't see how I could handle a three-week tour overseas.

I didn't have to go. How I thank Jesus for his love and

care. The tour was canceled for several unexpected reasons, and since I had no other appointments scheduled, I have three weeks' vacation. Friends offered me their very comfortable cabin in the mountains, and I came "home" to the trees, the squirrels, and the birds— and to a crackling fireplace. Elisabeth is spending her three vacation weeks with me, and my children and staff members come and go as their time permits.

We had some freak snowstorms, so I am spending most of my time in front of a big fire in the coziness of a soft rocking chair, reading, thinking, or communicating with my Lord. Elisabeth and I have had some long deep talks, too.

She is such a fine Bible scholar and has insights into the cultural settings of both the Old and the New Testaments which help me greatly.

The divorce and remarriage issue has been pressing on my mind for some time now. It isn't only for my sake that I need to understand it, it's for the people who come to me for advice and help. I do get now and then some irate letters which plainly condemn me. Usually some Bible texts are quoted out of context to prove that I am outside of the will of God because I am divorced. I am advised, scolded, threatened, and told a foolproof way to restore my marriage. Usually I don't answer such mail. My American dad or one of my staff members does. I don't feel any burden to defend myself. My burden is to help people.

Whether remarriage is right or wrong is not one of my personal concerns either—but I need to know for the sake of others who are in deep conflict over it.

I shall never forget the moment when I was introduced to Mark a few months ago. (That's not his real name, of course.) We were fellow speakers at a weekend conference, and I was a bit nervous about it. He is a very well-known speaker and writer, and I had been a fan of his for a long time. When we met, I was struck by the lines of deep suffering which I have learned to recognize in a human face.

I remarked about it to a mutual friend of ours. "I have never seen a kinder face," I said to her, "but there is incredible pain in it. That man hurts."

"He does," Monica answered. "He just went through a cruel, devastating divorce and this is his first time to speak again. He had vowed he'd *never* go up to a pulpit again."

I buried my face in my hands. "Lord, not him, too," I said, fighting tears. "He loved his wife and family so deeply. It comes through so clearly in his books."

I ached as I listened to him. I promised to pray for him when we parted after the last meeting.

We met just recently again at another convention. We had been scheduled as co-speakers and didn't know about it until the last moment. Somehow we managed to find an hour for personal talk, uninterrupted, very late in the evening. We were both exhausted.

I don't think Christian people realize how hard they can make life on public figures. They don't think of it, but it takes tremendous energy to give a sermon or speech. According to one statistic I read, a thirty-minute speech takes as much or more energy than eight hours of manual labor. It is not unusual for a minister or speaker to give more than three or four days of work energy during one day of heavy public speaking. I am drained after every meeting. I always give it *all* that I have in me. After a meeting, people come for counsel, prayer, or just to chat, and they take hours of a speaker's time without much thought or consideration of his or her personal welfare.

Mark and I talked about this problem while we sat together that evening. As I listened to him, I learned that a Christian man seems to have a different set of difficulties than a woman does.

We had in common that Mark gets condemning remarks and letters just as I do. Some of the cancellations

he has received were downright cruel. "Wherever they let
me speak, I quote your saying often," he said with a tired
smile.

"Which saying?" I asked.

"We Evangelicals are the only group who shoot their
wounded!" he said. "The painful truth of that has never
come home to me more than in the last few months since
I went back to speaking again. People can be cruel,
thoughtless, and almost vindictive at times. On the other
hand, I have my hands full trying to keep away the
women who feel called to comfort me."

We both laughed when I assured him that he was perfectly safe with me.

Mark turned serious. "I never dreamed that I would
ever be caught in a deep theological dilemma. Aside from
the fact that I don't desire to fool around with any woman
who would make herself available, don't I have a right to
find a good Christian companion for the rest of my life?"

I had true concern for him as I shared his hurts. He
was a brother in Christ who had served God by writing
and speaking for many years. He looked tired, defeated,
and he groped for answers. He didn't look like a person
who could stand to be alone for very long. I knew I had
no answers and I said so. I promised I would pray for him
and about the whole issue. We agreed to pray for each
other. We prayed together before we left.

I have done a lot of thinking about Mark's words. Does
he have God's permission to remarry or does he not?
Would I have a right to marry again as a person who sets
an example in Evangelical circles, or must I forfeit my
right simply because I am so well-known? I have no
plans, prospects, or even hopes to do so, but that could
change someday. I have avoided books on that subject so
far. I stay clear of things which I can't handle.

There was a time when I couldn't face the issue of Nazi
concentration camps. I couldn't talk about them. I never
read a book about them. I couldn't even say the words.

God brought Corrie ten Boom into my life to heal me and take that skeleton out of my closet.

Had God let me cross my path with Mark's so that I wouldn't any longer avoid what had been unsolved in my own mind? I know all the key texts that people write to me when they try to straighten my life out. I have read them over and over. I have prayed and meditated. I have asked God to show me clearly where my duties are. God always tells me, "You are free. You are mine. Trust me. I want to use you mightily."

I know that every person and each divorce case is different. No two breakups are alike. Is there one formula for approaching the issue as a whole, or must every case be approached individually? Is there one rule to be applied when a person is in public life and another to be applied to the average member of a Christian church?

Elisabeth and I spent hours in research, studying the Bible, praying, and talking. One evening I said to her, "You have never been married or divorced, neither is there any divorce in your immediate family. Your parents were participating church people and had a good marriage. What is your interpretation of the Scripture on that subject?"

Elisabeth seemed to have been waiting for that question. She had her books and Bible commentaries ready, and we settled down before the warm fireplace for an evening of discussion and friendly sharing.

She first went to the Old Testament texts that Christ referred to. In order to understand them, she said, one must consider the role of the woman in Jewish law and in Christ's time. A woman was not a person but a possession. A man could get rid of her for the most insignificant reasons: if she was a bad cook or if she found no more favor in his eyes. Only the man could divorce; the woman had no rights whatsoever. The Jewish society not only denied the woman equal rights, but if she was found in adultery, the man went free and the woman was stoned.

Jesus very obviously tried to do two things: he tried to put women into a place where they were respected as persons, and he tried to tighten up the easy divorce laws. But he did not annul them!

God had never intended divorce for his children. The biblical picture of marriage parallels his relationship to Israel and to his church. Divorce spoils God's object lesson to the world about his deep love for his children. It is never his will, but neither is any other problem or sin which dishonors him.

What God has put together, let no man put asunder.

Has every marriage been put together by *God?* Hardly! If two people seek the will of God and his approval and then receive his blessing, then you can say God put that marriage together. But even in those cases one partner may, by an act of his or her will, decide to follow temptation and forsake the marriage vow. God will not *force* that person to straighten up for the other partner's sake. Must the other party then be punished forever, too? Must God be forced to approve marriages he has not ordained in the first place?

Christ states very clearly the approval of divorce and remarriage in the case of adultery. What *all* is included in adultery? God calls Israel adulterous often when they have left him and followed other gods. Did he punish them forever when they left him?

God forgives *any* sin, if his children come to him and ask for forgiveness. He restored Israel to himself over and over, even after the most hideous sins.

God never gives conditional forgiveness. He always forgives *completely.* He forgives and forgets. If God forgets, we as children can live as though the sin never happened. We can have a completely new beginning. Divorce and adultery are no exceptions. Nowhere in the Bible does God make divorce the unpardonable sin. Only self-righteous legalists tend to consider it as such.

I listened to Elisabeth and watched the dying embers in

the fireplace. I saw faces in the shadows of the living room and heard in my heart the words of people in the past who had asked me for help with their deep conflicts.

I put my head on my knees and cried. I said, "Elisabeth, if what you just said is true, and I believe it is, then the greatest cruelty and injustice in the church is done to those who need her love, help, and forgiveness the *most*. The tragedy is that church saints do such inhuman judging in the name of our loving Christ!"

JUNE/ *Monday Morning*

I am so grateful for the three weeks of rest I had. My summer schedule is full and heavy. Between speaking appointments I seem to do more and more counseling.

One man came to me and asked me for a few minutes of my time. He told me a story I had heard before in similar words. He was a Christian doctor and was well-known in his community and state. He had been very active in his church, too. He and his wife had several children and seemed to have a happy home.

"She yelled at me for years," the troubled man said. "She told me that I seemed eager to have an affair with other women and that I had better go ahead and have it. It finally happened," he continued, and looked down. "I had sex with my office nurse who had come to me for advice. I felt rotten and completely repulsed afterward. I went to my wife and asked for her forgiveness. She screamed, yelled, and went hysterical, but she never forgave me. She called everyone she knew and told them of my sin. She called all over the state. Everybody in my church heard about it and avoided me. I confessed my sin before the pastor and the elders and asked for forgiveness. I asked the nurse for forgiveness. I went before God in deep repentance, but it seems that nobody, even yet, will forgive me. I know I did a foolish thing and made a mistake.

"My wife asked for a divorce and cleaned me out financially. She got everything I had. I don't mind that I am broke, but I do mind that I am not allowed to serve God any longer. They took all my church offices away from me; they won't let me teach the juniors in Sunday school anymore. I am a marked man.

"What bothers me the most is that our head elder lives in sin and he gets away with it. That nurse came to me for help because she wanted to get out of a relationship with him. It bothered her conscience. I got so emotionally involved when I tried to help her that I fell into it myself. Why does God let that man serve when I can't anymore? Am I condemned forever? Can I never marry again?"

I told the doctor what I thought, and assured him that God had forgiven him. I advised him to move his church membership and start all over in another church, since his own couldn't forgive and forget.

"Find a church that has a good program for singles," I said. "Trust God that he can bring beauty out of ashes."

How often I say these Bible words lately! "God *will* bring beauty out of ashes!"

That night I talked to God about that Christian brother who had come to me for counsel. "Jesus," I said, "did I have a right to say what I said? After all, it was a case of adultery. That's pretty serious, isn't it?"

The Lord said to me, "She *still* lives in spiritual adultery. He has repented."

"Spiritual adultery?" I asked, puzzled.

"Yes," God said. "She left and rejected *me* long before the whole thing happened. He made a mistake and I forgave him. She never came back to me and will have committed adultery, until she repents."

"Jesus," I said, "does adultery always begin with leaving you first?"

"Yes," my Lord said. "One has to first move out of the center of *my* will before he or she does any sin. Adultery is not just the sex act; adultery begins long before that!"

"I know," I nodded. "You said in the Bible that if

someone *looks* with lust in his *eyes*, he has already committed that sin. But, Lord, who then *is* without sin?''

"Nobody," the Lord said, "that's why I told my children not to judge. Remember what I showed you and
Elisabeth in the cabin while you searched and prayed?''

"You showed us so much, Jesus," I said, "that I still try
to digest it all. What is it in connection with this matter?"

"You tried to figure out the difference between the laws
of Moses and my New Testament commandments," the
Lord reminded me. "Remember what you both discovered?''

"How can I ever forget?" I said with joy in my heart.
"It was the most exciting discovery of the three weeks.
The Jews kept every law as an act, but your commandments are attitudes and motives, not acts. The actions
come as a result of the attitude, don't they?"

"Right, my child," the Lord said. "And at my Judgment Day some church people will be surprised when the
true hearts of men are revealed. Many bright stars in the
church sky will suddenly have lost their shine, and their
secret lives will not be hidden any longer. Many so-called
sinners and rejected people will be justified, honored, and
vindicated because their true hearts were right although
they made mistakes."

"Lord," I said, "if people can remarry after they have
committed adultery or their home has broken up for other
reasons, could you give me an example of it in the
Bible?''

I have done this before—asked Jesus for a concrete
example in the Bible, when I wasn't completely sure of
something. I remember when I asked him for a biblical
example just before I filed for divorce. According to the
legalistic interpretation of the Bible I went against biblical
principles, even as I understood them at that time.

"Show me a Bible story," I pleaded then, "which
shows a person seemingly going against the commonly
understood laws of God of his time."

"Abraham," God answered. "Abraham knew my law concerning human sacrifice. He also knew that the heathen of the land sacrificed their children to their idols. He knew I abhorred the practice. But he knew my voice and therefore he obeyed me when I gave him that humanly impossible command. He *did* take Isaac and he intended to sacrifice him on the altar without rationalizing with me. He trusted *me*—not my laws, not my promises alone, and not the interpretations of his heart."

Now Jesus did it again! He gave me an example of God's complete forgiveness and how he will forget the pasts of a sinner: "David! King David! The sweet singer of psalms, the man of war who carried blood on his hands, the adulterer who got a married woman pregnant and killed her husband to cover his own sin."

"Lord," I said, "I have read somewhere that David as the king of Israel had the right to *any* woman or man in his kingdom. Therefore he probably wasn't aware of the gravity of his sin. When the prophet came to show it to him, he was so unaware that he even wanted to kill the man who had done such a miserable thing!"

"That is so," the Lord said, "but remember that *I change not.* Sin is sin regardless of cultural factors. And if the sin of adultery or murder were unpardonable, I wouldn't have pardoned King David. He made some grave mistakes in his life, but his attitudes and motives were usually *right.* The moment he saw his sin, he repented and asked for forgiveness and cleansing. I did what he asked for and I put his transgressions away. Remember, I *blessed* his marriage with Bath-sheba so much that *she* gave him the heir to the throne, King Solomon."

I went to sleep that night overwhelmed by the love and mercy of my Lord. I have a great desire to help people see the love of God and what is the truly important thing in our relationship to him: our attitudes and motives!

Since nobody can know a person's *true* motives, we have no right to judge or decide for them.

One woman came up to me after a retreat. I had
touched on the issue of divorce in connection with my
Black Sheep message and, as always, it had left the audience shaken and in tears.

"You mean I have to give my approval to my brother
who is planning his second marriage next week?" she
growled.

"Did he ask you for your approval?" I said gently.

Her face turned cold. "No," she said, and her fingers
clutched the chair so hard that her knuckles turned white.
"No," she growled again. "He knew I would *never* give
my approval."

"My dear, I don't think it is any of your business to decide if your brother can remarry or not. That is something
between God, him, and his future wife. Nobody else can
make the final decision but those three." I said it as kindly
as possible.

"You mean I should go to the wedding?" she said de-
fensively.

"What are you trying to prove by staying away?" I
asked.

"Someone must stand up for what is *right* in God's
eyes and in his Word. God condemns remarriage! So I
show on which side I stand when I stay away. I didn't
even go to my children's weddings when they remarried."

I looked at my sister in the Lord. She looked so pale,
bitter, and miserable while defending the "laws" of the
Lord. "Honey," I said, and I ached so badly I fought my
ever-ready tears again, "I hesitate to tell you this, but I
believe that we parents don't even have a right to tell our
own grown children what to do and what not to do. We
must let go and let God! All we can do is stand by and
love them, even if they make a mistake. Our censoring
and judging spirit will only drive people deeper into their
own and perhaps wrong convictions." I looked at her and
smiled. "Did you ever read in the Bible what the fulfillment of the law is?"

She looked blank. I smiled more widely. "*Love* is the fulfillment of the law! If we keep any law for any other motive or reason but because we love God and others as ourselves, we are not keeping his commandments. We break them, although we are standing on the right side. Ask yourself a question: do you stay away from such weddings because you love the couple, or because you want to prove your own 'holier-than-thou' attitude? Have you *helped* anyone so far by staying away?"

"No!" she said hoarsely. "I haven't helped anything. Everyone gets married anyway, even if I don't come. My children and I are not even on speaking terms. *I am so alone!*" Her face softened and tears began to flow.

"Why don't you go to your children and to your brother and ask them for forgiveness for your judgmental attitude and see what God will do to restore your broken relationships? Don't deprive your family of your love just because they are not interpreting the Bible the way you do."

"I don't know if I can do that," she said, looking terrified. "After all, I know that I am *right,* but . . ."

"Honey," I said, "promise me one thing. Pray about it and ask Jesus to show you what to do. Can you at least do that much?"

"Yes," she said, "I'll go home and pray about it." She got up and said good-bye. As she turned, she murmured to herself, "I don't think it's right to go to his wedding, but I'll pray about it."

She walked away and I felt great relief. At least she would pray about it, she had said. And if she wanted to do God's will, he would lead her, one step at a time. I was sure of that.

I can't forget the face of that woman. I had a question about it. I wonder how she would look if she smiled? She didn't smile at me—not even once. "Lord, please teach her about your love and forgiveness," I prayed in my heart. "Teach *all* of us!"

JULY/ *Sunday Night*

The motors of the jet hum their familiar tune. I am on my way home and can't wait to get there. I want to see my children.

Summer speaking is rough, especially this summer. Wherever I went, east or west, there was a heat wave. Most high school auditoriums have no air-conditioning, and the outdoor places don't cool off fast enough. It always amazes me that the people come in spite of the heat. Maybe they come because of it. People begin to wonder if the weather is just a quirk of nature or if God is letting it happen for a very special reason.

I believe that the drought is God's way of warning a country. Severe weather conditions of any kind are permitted by God to draw the attention of the people to the wickedness of their land.

I see my beloved homeland America eaten and devoured by sin. This beautiful Christian nation is losing her vision and the people perish. I am deeply concerned— and I say so. The reason why I agree to speak in the summer, when most ministries and speakers take a vacation, is the urgency of the hour. We need to get to God's children before it is too late to reverse the trend of American life. We also need to get to the Christian communities in Canada. These countries are like twin brothers. They quibble all the time, but what one does always affects the other profoundly. I see both nations heading in the same direction—toward destruction and God's punishment. The last two signs before any place or country goes into judgment are people turning to the occult, and to sex perversion. I never thought that I would see America turn to such wickedness.

Nazi Germany was based on devil worship and I recognize the signs when I see them. Yoga, transcendental meditation, and all those other fancy meditations are new names for an old deception of Satan. It's sweeping the

Western World like a wildfire and the people can't see it. I can—and I speak up about it. I ask the audiences to pray. A prayer revival, a great new awakening toward the spiritual things of God, is our country's *only* chance of survival.

If people only knew what prayer can do! Some begin to find out. As prayer groups have begun to form across this land, we get reports and letters which tell of God's willingness to answer. We also see God's miraculous power and his special protection over those who speak out against wickedness.

I know that I wouldn't be alive anymore if it weren't for God's sovereign will and the many prayers which are said in my behalf. I shall never forget the night I spoke up against the occult while on tour in Florida. It was last winter, and our hostess had forgotten to make motel reservations early enough. We ended up in a bungalow-type motel beside a busy highway. We left that place one late afternoon to drive quite a distance to a church where I spoke for an evening meeting. God's Spirit was very evident, and I emphasized prayer and the forming of prayer groups as a spiritual weapon against Satan and the occult. After the meeting a group of church people came to talk to me.

"Do you mean to say that our prayers could drive the evil forces out of our town?" one woman asked. "An occult movement has just bought two of the largest buildings downtown as their new headquarters. You mean our prayer could affect their stay?"

I smiled and nodded. "It surely can, my friends. I spoke just the other day by telephone with a friend of mine. She told me that they've had an overwhelming victory over the forces of darkness in their city. One occult organization was negotiating with the city administration about buying a large training center which was up for sale. Some Christians found out about it. They activated their prayer groups and telephone prayer chains everywhere, and then prayed faithfully, pleading the blood of Christ and his power over their city. The negotiations failed. One Christian man knew someone of that occult organization and asked why they pulled out of the deal. He was told that they didn't feel 'at ease' in the place anymore; too many opposing 'vibes' were suddenly coming their way.

"I am sorry you let Satan get a foothold," I said to the group. "It's easier when we Christians are alert enough to stop evil things before they can root and grow. But don't give up. Get your prayer forces together and attack the enemy. Make it so uncomfortable for the demonic powers that they *want* to leave."

After giving the Christians some suggestions and ideas on how to form effective prayer groups and telephone chains, we left for our long drive back to the motel. We arrived around midnight, and I felt weary and exhausted. The elderly minister, his wife, Mary, and I made our way quickly to our adjoining rooms. On our door was a big note. "Please do not enter. Come to the office."

Mary and the minister did so while I waited before the door, praying. "Lord," I said, "what is it? Did anything happen to any of my children?" My children are never far from my heart, and they are my first and last prayer request every day. I try hard not to worry about them, but in any emergency they are always my first thought.

The motel owner came back with the minister and Mary. He looked very apologetic and tired. "I didn't want you to enter your room unless you were forewarned," he said to me. "It's a total mess and you can't sleep in it. Shortly after you left this afternoon, an elderly woman driving along this highway lost control, and her car plowed right through the brick wall into your room. I don't know why it had to be *your* room," he said. "In some of the other rooms it wouldn't have done so much damage, because people had checked out and others had not moved in yet."

He opened the door. I looked around by the aid of his

flashlight, since all the power lines had been cut. I couldn't believe my eyes. "I *know* why it had to be my room," I murmured. "I understand it *very* well!"

"We took some of your clothing out of the closet and put it into the minister's room," the manager said. "We tried to get everything out because the place is open and subject to looting. As a matter of fact, the police arrested a looter shortly after the accident happened."

"What happened to the driver?" I said.

"It took forty-five minutes to pry her and her passenger out of the wreck," he answered. He wiped his brow. "What a day this was! Oh, what a day! Both are in the hospital on the critical list, but expected to live."

The situation suddenly hit me, and I looked through the rubble, picking up strewn pieces that had been thrown out of our open suitcases. "Where is my brief-case?" I asked, and cold panic gripped me for a moment.

Everyone looked blank. "We haven't seen any brief-case," the owner said. "I am sure we tried to get all we could out of the room, but I can't recall finding a brief-case."

"I have a nearly completed handwritten book manu-script in it," I said and tried to keep my voice calm. "I had to carry it with me becaue I have no other time to write but while I travel. If that manuscript is lost, I can nev-er. replace it. I would have a hard time recalling all of it; I spent nearly a year working on it in my spare time." I had a hard time keeping my composure. I felt too tired to cope, too discouraged even to comprehend the thought of starting to write all over.

Mary had worked her way through the cement blocks and rubble toward the closet door. She opened it and shined her flashlight into the dark emptiness. "There it is!" she said triumphantly. "I was pretty sure I had put it in there before we left." She handed it to me and I cried with relief.

"I don't care what else is lost," I said, smiling through

tears, "as long as the manuscript is here. Thank you, Lord!"

The motel owner shook his head. "Ma'am," he said, "you are luckier than you realize! We had three fire trucks here because the wreck had cut a gas line. We expected an explosion and a fire. When my wife tried to get your clothing, a fireman tried to stop her. She went in anyway to save your stuff. She never saw that briefcase, though."

"The closet door was open when we left," Mary said. "I remember distinctly that I thought of it, wondering if I should close it. When we went out the door, we were in such a hurry that I didn't go back to do it."

"The closet door was shut when we entered," the man said. "The impact of the air pressure must have pushed the briefcase into the farthest corner and closed the door."

I smiled and nodded. Maybe it *was* air pressure that did it when the whole wall was pushed in and the cement blocks flew through the room. Maybe it wasn't! God's angels have moved more than briefcases for me in my life!

We had another problem that night. We had no beds to sleep in. Every hotel in town was full. Even the one where we stayed simply had no bed to offer. A guest who had rented a whole suite and had heard about the accident offered us the spare couch in her sitting room. We accepted it without hesitation. We were ready to drop!

By noon the next day we were able to move into another room. We found all our stuff, some of it scratched or damaged, but nothing in such a way that it couldn't be replaced or repaired in a short time. As we sifted through the dust and mess, Mary looked up and said, "I can't shake a picture before my inner eye. I see you lying on your tummy on the bed right next to the wall where the car crashed through. The owner said this morning that the accident happened no more than ten minutes after we left."

I looked at the bed I had lain on, praying, before we left. It was covered with bricks and debris. The car had shoved it out of the way toward the next bed. I might never have spoken that night—or ever again—if we hadn't left when we did.

Yes, I wouldn't be able to do anything, either in the winter or this summer or in spring or fall or any year if it were not for God's triumphant power and protection over me.

"Why do you speak up against the occult and satanic things when you *know* that it brings Satan's special wrath upon a person to do so?" one church saint asked me when I told the story in a prayer meeting on this last tour. "Aren't we doing enough when we protect ourselves by prayer and the blood of Christ? Aren't you *afraid* of what could happen to you or your children if you don't stop antagonizing the devil? Aren't you *asking* deliberately for trouble?"

"Am I asking for trouble, Lord?" I am looking out the little window beside my plane seat. We are up in the deep blue sky. I like to fly. I feel closer to God in the air than on the ground. I should! If my plane did go down, I would be very close to God and arrive "home" faster than I anticipate right now.

The longer I walk and talk with the Lord, the clearer I see the great conflict between Christ and Satan. Satan is a powerful foe, that I know by now.

But I know something else, too: Jesus Christ *is* stronger. He *is* Victor and he has told us to go and attack the powers and demons of hell. We Christians are engaged in spiritual warfare, not in retreat or defense alone.

"The best defense is offense," my American dad, a former officer and trainer of the Reserve forces, told me once. He should know, he helped prepare American troops for World War I.

Yes, I'd rather be on the offense than defense when it comes to the occult. I have a personal account to settle with the great enemy of souls. He stole from me what was dearest to my heart.

I shall be wrestling with the dark powers unto heaven and trust my Jesus. The battle is his and I am not afraid.

I came from the side which lost the last two world wars. I am so glad I finally joined the *winning* side.

Someday the kingdoms of this world will all become the kingdom of my Lord and he will reign forever and ever. We, who are engaged in HIS warfare, shall then be with HIM. I can't wait!

AUGUST/ *Saturday Night*

Home at last for vacation. This was another full, work-filled month, but a good one! God is overwhelmingly good to me. He honors me beyond anything I could ever think or ask for.

I received a very special award this month. I can hardly remember the fancy name of it! Distinguished Service Citation. The organization which selected me for it has given that honor to seventeen people in the last ninety-three years. I found myself in the company of such distinguished names as Admiral Richard Byrd, Dr. Kenneth Taylor, and President Herbert Hoover.

I stood at the podium when they handed me the big plaque and wondered if it was all a dream. Hundreds of flash bulbs flashed and cameras hummed and clicked endlessly. Several thousands of young Christian delegates from all over the world stood and whistled and clapped. I stood in a daze and wondered if I would be able to say anything. My heart felt like it would burst with my deep gratitude to God, and the tears streamed down my face.

I remembered a similar occasion a few months earlier. It all began so simply. I had a Saturday luncheon appointment to speak for a meeting of the Daughters of the American Revolution. I hadn't given it much thought except that I felt honored to speak for such a distinguished group. What a thrill it would be, I thought, to be able to trace one's lineage back to those brave God-fearing, patriotic men who made America and freedom a reality!

"Do they know that I am a *Christian* speaker?" I asked Mary as we discussed the schedule for that particular week. "I don't know what their philosophy is, but I don't intend to alter my message."

"You don't have to," Mary said. "Some in the group are Christians and some are not. All of them are very patriotic. The lady who made the arrangements goes to my church. She knows your message. She heard you speak before; that's why she wants you to speak to them. She believes that your message is something her group would appreciate and cherish."

I should have realized that something special was brewing, but I didn't. The *Los Angeles Times* sent out a friendly reporter to interview me about my work. A TV network asked for a half-hour special. Another leading newspaper called in for a feature article. I was jubilant. "It looks as if the news media are suddenly interested in Christian patriotism," I said to my staff people in the office. "Isn't it remarkable how all of a sudden everyone is so interested in what our ministry is trying to do?"

Everyone acted nonchalant and I behaved as usual, like a naive, dumb girl from the hayloft who never suspects anything.

Two days before the luncheon I had a board meeting to attend. I dislike committee and board meetings. I can never figure out the correct procedure, and motions and second motions make me squirm in my chair. I felt uncomfortable as usual when Dr. Walters, the president, called the meeting to order.

When he is my American dad, I enjoy being with him. When he becomes the president, I feel out of place and want to get the meeting behind me. I wanted to do more than that when he announced that I would receive the

Medal of Americanism from the Daughters of the American Revolution. It was, he said, the highest national award for a naturalized citizen of the United States. My first reaction was panic. I felt my heart skip a beat. "Lord," I thought, "what will I *do* or *say* if they give me such an honor?"

Dr. Walters gave me one look and realized he had spilled the beans. "Oh, dear," he said, "was I not supposed to tell?"

The board members nodded gravely, and I was stunned for the rest of the meeting. I had just one wish; I needed to go home and have some time alone with God.

While I sat through the rest of our agenda I suddenly figured out why the press had shown up and several of my best friends had called and announced a surprise visit for the weekend. It had puzzled me no end why everyone seemed to descend on me the same weekend, when I had neither a birthday or any other special day to celebrate.

When I finally got away from the meeting and the many other demands which fill my days, I had the needed quiet hour with my Lord. "Jesus," I said, "you know how scared I am. I don't know how to handle such a thing. Furthermore, I don't think I *deserve* such a medal. I haven't done anything special. You know that if I did any good, you did it through me!"

I could see the Lord smile before my inner eye when he answered, "Well, my child, if you don't want to receive any honor for yourself because you don't deserve it, why don't you go and receive it for *me* instead. I'll go with you to receive it, and I will give you the words to say. I'll also help you to control your ever-ready tears."

That's exactly what happened at the luncheon when they handed me that obviously very rare medal. Jesus was there, right beside me, and I received it for him. I said so and I cried a bit, and the honored guests gave me a standing ovation, Christians and non-Christians alike.

One grand old decorated lady came up after it was all over and the flash bulbs, congratulatory hugs, and kisses had settled down. She said, "What you said to us needed to be said to every American. You reminded us of our Christian heritage. We have forgotten that Christianity and patriotism go together."

"Yes, ma'am," I said quietly, "and if America ever forgets what made her so great and special, she will go under like every other nation. Your forefathers who fought in the American Revolution understood it well— faith in God and freedom had to go hand in hand. Freedom is built upon the inner control which comes from the restraints of the Christian ethic. If the American people ever let go of that inner control, they will be inviting the outer control of dictatorship."

"Thank you for reminding me that we still *are* a nation under God," the lady said and wiped her eyes. "It's so easy to forget, so easy to take it all for granted."

When I received the special citation this month, I told the young people about that incident. I made it very clear that I accepted the international award for my Lord and Master Jesus Christ only. "I owe him everything! Without him I could do nothing! All the glory, honor, and credit must go to him alone. He is the One who has done everything that is worthy of human recognition in my life."

The Lord, the young people, the leaders of the convention, and I had a great evening together. Sure, it was hot. It was so hot and humid that all of us steamed.

Before I gave the main address, I assured everybody that being in a huge auditorium without air-conditioning in 102° heat in 94 percent humidity was only an inconvenience. It becomes a hardship if one faints! "Let's not complain," I said. "We are so fortunate that we are all able to gather here in freedom tonight. The provisions for us this evening are actually things which even in America only rich people can afford. They pay much money to have it built. They call it a sauna!"

The young people shouted with laughter and clapped wildly. What a joy we all had! What fellowship! What love! The whole month has been so extra full with joyful happenings. It's almost as though Jesus is filling me with a special strength which comes out of such happy experiences. I wonder if he is preparing me for something?

SEPTEMBER/ *Friday Night*

Yes, my Lord was preparing me for something—something special and very hard.

My American dad died right at the beginning of our family vacation. He had a heart attack a few weeks before his death and though it was serious, he had begun to improve and get better. At least, we thought so.

My children and I saw him in the hospital before I had to leave for a short weekend trip. A meeting had been rained out in Missouri and I had to go back during my vacation to keep that commitment.

The telephone call reached me before I ever got to the pulpit to speak. I remembered what he had said to us before we left him on our last visit.

"Find out where your talents and abilities are, then give it your very best and work hard to develop them. Be true to God and to yourself. . . ."

It was a farewell speech and we all knew it. But we smiled and never acknowledged it to each other. I couldn't even admit it to myself.

I wondered how I could speak twice the day after that call had reached me. My loss was so great I couldn't cry.

I spoke! I knew that my dad expected me to speak if I wanted to honor his memory. God helped me to forget how raw and alone I felt, how desperately alone! Twice I spoke and it was my double tribute for one of God's great servants.

I didn't speak about him. I spoke about Jesus and my

great love and concern about America. Dad would have
wanted it that way. He didn't like it when people were
glorified, even after they died. All the glory must always
go where it belongs—to God alone.

God was his first and great love. To serve others was
right next to it. Because he had his priorities straight God
blessed him and made him to prosper. My children
learned much from him, especially my two sons.

I will never forget the time when we had gone out together. The grandparents were treating us to a very special dinner in one of their favorite restaurants. Dad looked
at Tim with a thoughtful expression and said, "You know,
when I retired I felt that I had paid my debt to society.
We were financially secure so I decided that in my old
age I could do what I wanted to do most: To help others
without charging anything to anybody."

I looked at the grand old man and marveled. He was
hard of hearing and had very poor eyesight. But he
worked for twelve to sixteen hours a day without pay,
and shared his tremendous business experience with
many ministries.

What an example he set for other senior citizens! When
I think of the many retired people who lose their zest and
vitality, and see themselves on a dead-end track. What a
loss to our society! What a waste to condemn old people
to a life of inactivity and uselessness.

It takes a whole lifetime to gain the experience they
possess. Why must the younger generation learn everything all over, if they could profit by the teachings and insights of the aged?

My dad didn't wait for society to come and *ask* for his
help—he gave it freely by his own initiative. He found
himself enough to do that he never had enough hours in
a day to do it all. Many retired people could find a full
and busy life if they were willing to do what they were
not able to do as long as they had to earn a living: To do
something for the sheer joy of helping and working with-

out a thought of pay. That's what my dad did and he had
some special rewards. He saw many of God's ministries
prosper and become financially stable because he set
them up soundly.

He would often talk to me about it. "Why do Christians
think they can fumble along and God will bless anything
they do just because it is God's work." He would shake
his wise head. "Doesn't God deserve the best of everything, even in a business setup?"

Whatever he did, he did to the utmost of his ability and
God blessed his unselfish efforts. How he was used in our
ministry alone, besides so many others, only eternity will
show. What I would have done without him I cannot im-
agine.

Even the transition of leadership in our young organization had been prepared ahead of time by him and the
Lord. Dad had resigned four months before his death
from the presidency and our board had called Elisabeth
as the new president and administrator. She had begun to
work full-time for us by the beginning of this month.

During the summer months Dad had made a very de-
liberate attempt to lay the leadership of the ministry in a
most methodical way into Elisabeth's hands. We had no
harsh or damaging adjustments to make when the blow
came. God had foreseen the emergency.

My children and I sat with Mother and her immediate
family. I felt so grateful that we were permitted to do so. I
had never been at any funeral for a close family member
before. Now I know how stunned, numb and, on the
other hand, peaceful in God one can feel when they close
a casket. I knew that part of my heart would be buried,
too.

"Mom," Kathy asked, "why did God give us a grandpa
just to take him away so soon?"

"Let's not see it that way, honey," I said quietly. "Let's
thank God that he did give him to us for a few short
years. It is better to have had him and suffer now under
the loss than never to have known him. I know now what

a father is. I never had one like him ever before in my whole life. You children grew up without grandparents. Now you know what deep influence they can have on young lives."

Brother Andrew, "God's smuggler," had flown in from Holland to give the eulogy. Corrie ten Boom gave the prayer.

As I listened to them, I had to think of Moses, my favorite Bible character. When Moses' work was done, God told him to climb a mountain. He obeyed and Jesus stood waiting for him at the mountaintop.

I know that the last few weeks before Dad died, he also climbed God's mountain. With shortened breath and great effort he worked and served to the last moment. When he reached the top, the Lord stood there, waiting with outstretched arms.

Tante Corrie said it so fittingly in her prayer: "Death was his gain and our loss."

We do not sorrow as those who have no hope, but what a void he left!

Our entire vacation was overshadowed by Dad's death. But God is so good, and he finds happy surprises for his mourning children.

Just a week after the funeral he brought our Tina to us for a visit. Three of the children hadn't seen her and her husband for at least six years. Tina had not been in contact with me since the divorce. I had shed many tears about it. I understood why she felt bitter and defensive.

On her last birthday I had sent her another birthday card. I had asked her to forgive me. I knew I had made the most mistakes with her. I not only forced too much religion down her throat and tried to box her into my unbending legalistic concepts, I had asked too much of her as a child. She had to carry too many responsibilities from a very young age. "I cannot change the past," I wrote, "as much as I would love to do so. But I can ask you to forgive me and pray that God will make it up to you."

They came to see me for a happy afternoon on their

way to Hawaii. We had a steak cookout in the backyard, and we talked and laughed a lot. I cannot believe that my children did all the mischievous things they teased each other about! I know I am naive, but I never dreamed I was that unsuspecting a mother!

When Tina and her husband left, we all saw them to the airport. She kissed me good-bye and said, "Come and see us, Mother."

I promised I would. Another cloud had been rolled away by love and forgiveness. How I thank God!

After Tina's visit the children began to plan for the new school year. Tim is entering his senior year. It will be the hardest, since he will have a senior project to complete, Kathy and Heidi are still at the same college. Peter is another senior—at a Christian high school.

The days before we all parted, I sensed that the kids wanted to share something with me. Tim was obviously appointed to break the news to me. In a friendly conversation, he said ever so lightly, "By the way, we might soon have another member added to our family."

I looked up, puzzled. "What do you mean?" I said. "Is anyone expecting a baby?"

"No, Dad and Diane announced their official engagement and wedding date. We celebrated the engagement last weekend with them at the restaurant near our former cabin." Tim never took his clear blue eyes off me while he spoke.

I winced only one tiny bit and hoped he couldn't see it. But I am afraid he did. His face clouded over. I smiled big. "I hope they'll be happy," I said. "I have been praying for a long time for her, and him, of course. I hope they can give each other what they desire."

Tim and the others changed the subject and began to discuss their school plans again.

How I thank God for my children. They are rather protective of me, thoughtful and eager not to hurt me unnecessarily—but certain hurts we cannot keep out. We must learn to face them, live with them, and trust God that he can grow flowers because tears wet the soil of our heart. This vacation should produce a whole flower garden!

OCTOBER/ *Sunday Morning*

I have a Sunday afternoon meeting, so I tried to sleep in, this morning. I am tired. Last night people partied in the room next to us. It is happening more and more that staying in even the best hotels becomes difficult, particularly over the weekends. People who don't drink do not fit the social pattern of the present time very well.

This morning the same noisy gang of young men is leaving in such a way that the whole world must know they're leaving. Mary had tried to calm them down. She even called the front desk. I suggested that we just stay out of their way.

Well, I can't sleep anyway. I have some letters in my briefcase which need to be answered immediately. A pack of mail was waiting for me when we checked in yesterday afternoon. The office staff tries very hard to take care of the mail. Ever since Elisabeth began working full-time in the office, things have gotten so much easier for all of us. Cheri had her hands full and so did we. But certain mail cannot be opened by the office. If it is addressed to me personally or marked confidential, it is held or mailed unopened to me.

I read the mail last night. One letter has hit me right in the pit of my stomach. It made me cry with relief and joy. It came from a young woman—named Ellen. I met her at a retreat last year. She came with two other women, a mother and daughter. They drove 500 miles to attend the meetings. I went out for a cup of tea with all three of them after the first meeting and we talked. I should say three of us talked while Ellen looked at me and listened. I could sense a great defensiveness in her, a fear. She seemed imprisoned in her own dark world. I tried several times to include her in our conversation. I prayed silently for wisdom to find the right words to break through. It seemed hopeless.

She sat near the front in all the meetings and I watched her face, a sad face that never smiled.

I prayed much for that face. I asked God to use me in some way to help her. She listened very closely; her eyes were always on me whenever I looked at her.

After the last meeting people said good-bye to me. The three women had a long way to drive and so did we. I hugged each one of them and then looked into Ellen's face. "Honey," I said to her, "God has a *special* plan for your life."

For the first time I saw life come into her dark eyes. She almost smiled. Then the spark left again, and her face was as closed as ever. We waved to each other as they drove off.

A week later I had a long letter from Ellen. Her handwriting was very neat and showed high intelligence. Her ability to express herself was surprising to me, since she had hardly spoken when we met.

She challenged me. "You said that God has a special plan for my life," she wrote. "What do you mean by that? Do you tell that to everybody you meet?" She continued to assure me that I was greatly mistaken if I believed that God could use her, since she was a homosexual and therefore on the road to hell.

I answered that letter by return mail. I told her that I *could* tell anyone that God had a special plan for his or her life because it was true. Nevertheless, I don't say it to anybody unless God tells me to. I told her that I had prayed much for her because her sad face had gotten to me and God had told me that he has a special plan for her battered life. I also assured her that God loved her.

He condemns sin, but he loves sinners, and so do I. I
explained to her what I have written in so many letters
before: Our *first* step is to invite Jesus into our heart. We
give him our messed-up life and ask for forgiveness. After
Christ has come in and we are born again in the Spirit,
then Christ will do for us what we are not able to do by
ourselves: we overcome the sins and wrong habits of our
previous life.

Ellen and her companion did just that, and they told
me about it. I was delighted for both of them.

Ellen's next letter came like a lightning bolt out of the
blue sky. She asked if she would go to hell if she killed a
man. "It's the stepfather of one of my dearest friends,"
she wrote. "I hate him. He ruined her. He would tie her
up for days and nights, arms and legs spread apart—and
she was only twelve years old. He would hurt her so
badly that she still carries the scars of all the abuse on her
body. The girl's mother would come in and find her tied
up and would just laugh about it. That man must pay,"
Ellen wrote. "And I shall have no peace until he is sent to
hell."

I laid my head on top of her letter and sobbed. I ached
so badly for her—and all the thousands of other young
people who have been tortured and abused, and whose
lives have been crippled by merciless adults. I knew it
wasn't a friend of hers she tried to avenge, it was herself.
But she was too ashamed to admit it.

I wrote her a very long, hand-written letter and
explained to her where her thinking was wrong. I told her
that she was destroying herself, not that cruel man. If she
put him out of his misery, she didn't hurt only him, but
herself—and us, those who love her.

I told her that he might not know better. Maybe nobody had ever told him of Jesus and he might have
grown up in a terrible environment himself.

I showed her that the only way to break out of this

whole vicious circle would be by being willing to forgive. If she forgave by her will, Jesus could heal her—and perhaps begin some healing in other lives, too.

I mailed the letter myself, and the office sent Ellen's name with an indefinite request for her safety to all our prayer groups. I waited and prayed a lot for her. I knew she was in dead earnest about her plan, and I wondered if I would get her next letter from a prison.

It did not happen. The office mailed me her letter yesterday and I cried again—this time with joy. Ellen decided to forgive, and trust Jesus. She admitted that it was her own life's story. She also admitted that she had laid out the plan for how to get revenge. "Now I will let God handle it," she wrote. "And I feel like a new person. I still have a long way to go, and so much to learn, but I am willing!"

While the rock music blared from the next room last night, I wrote an answer to Ellen's letter. How I praise God for his strong power. Nobody but the Lord and his love can touch such a mishandled life as hers.

Lately I receive more and more mail from "gay" people of both sexes. Whenever I mention the occult and sex deviation as the last two sins before a nation goes under, they feel condemned.

One man wrote, "I cannot sleep or eat since I heard you speak. I am gay. Will I go to hell? Answer me immediately!"

I answered by return mail. I wrote: "Nobody goes to hell who accepts Jesus Christ as his Savior and Lord. Christ loves you. Nevertheless, we cannot call right what he declares wrong. Homosexuality is no *more* wrong than the other sins, but you must acknowledge your need for help and ask him to set you free."

He never wrote back. We put his name on our prayer lists.

Two girls approached me after a meeting in the Midwest last fall. They asked me if they could talk to me in private. We went from the foyer back into the semidarkened, empty sanctuary and sat down.

One girl took a deep breath. "We have been gay," she blurted out. "What do you think about us?"

"First of all, let me tell you that I love you!" I said. Both girls gave a deep sigh and their shoulders sagged. They began to relax and talk.

"We attended a meeting in the East where you spoke last spring," Shelly said. "We both accepted Christ. We try hard to live right, but we need help. We cannot find people who will help us to understand things. Can we ask you some questions?"

"You surely may," I said, "but keep in mind that I might not have all the answers."

"That's OK," Shelly said while Yvonne mostly nodded and listened. "But if we can just talk to someone, it might help.

"I don't need to ask you if homosexuality is wrong; the first chapter of Romans settled it for us after we began to read the Bible together. What I can't understand is why I still feel or desire to make love to her after Christ came into our lives. We have decided not to do it anymore." Both girls looked very troubled.

I smiled. "Girls, that is not only a 'gay' problem, but a sin problem. Regardless of what your body or soul wants that is wrong, after you are born again in the Spirit it takes a while for your souls and bodies to catch on that you are under a new rule—the Spirit's leadership.

"My friend Corrie ten Boom tells it this way: When a bell is pulled, it swings and rings. Your sex drive had you swinging wildly. You are not pulling on the bell anymore, but the inner clapper of the bell hasn't caught on yet. You will still get a few ding-dongs from the inside of your non-swinging bell."

"Is that a sin?" Yvonne asked.

"No, temptation is not sin. It leads you into sin when you begin playing with it, dwelling on it, and considering it. Martin Luther said that you cannot stop the blackbirds from flying over your head, but you can stop them from building nests in your hair." I smiled.

Shelly had another worry. "I am afraid we might slip someday and fall back into the old way of life. I worry much about it because I am the one who leads in this relationship."

"Our fears usually bring on what we are most afraid of," I said seriously. "And I know well what fear can do to a person. I have been tortured with fear most of my life, until I learned how to deal with it. Give your fears to Jesus every day. Ask him to protect you against yourself. Ask him to do it for you. He will! Should you ever fall, go to him and ask him to forgive and cleanse you and then get up and go on. Don't be so preoccupied with the sexual side of your life that you cannot see other areas where you need to overcome, grow, and mature.

"You must know that judging is just as wrong and as great a sin as homosexuality or premarital sex or sex perversions which are acted out within a legal marriage. Sin is sin. Like a cancer, it can afflict different areas of our whole being, but it is *always* malignant—unless Jesus heals us."

"Now I have one more question," Shelly said. "Why does Anita Bryant call us creeps and say that she hopes we all get the plague or scurvy and die? She claims to be a Christian. I know that some of the most sensitive, beautiful people live in the gay community. They don't bother anybody. They are faithful to each other, keep good jobs, help other people. They even go to church."

"First of all, remember that the press has a tendency to misquote people," I said. "I know it best. Several times I have been badly misquoted, and all one gets out of it afterward is an apology, but then the damage is done. I don't know what Anita really said. I don't know her personally. I just know a friend of hers. She told me that Anita realizes today that she began with the wrong approach. She fought sinners, not sin. We must *never* do that. We must always love any sinner as Jesus did. But we must condemn sin. We cannot whitewash, legalize, or call right what God calls wrong."

"We understand that," the girls nodded. "But why do Christians avoid us when we come to church? We gave our testimony once, but we wouldn't dare to do it again. We have been treated as though we carry a contagious disease ever since."

"Girls," I said, and I ached as I ache so often when I counsel and face the shortcomings of my own Christian community. "We Christians have so far no answers for the 'gays.' We don't know how to approach it. We are still arguing over whether it is really a hereditary problem, a congenital disease, or something that is learned by wrong environmental cues. I have no idea myself, as a psychologist, where to begin. All I know is that Christ has the answers. He is able to pull anyone out of anything, be it alcoholism, smoking, drug addiction, or wrong sex bonds of any kind.

"I need your help to comprehend your problem. Only as I begin to understand where your head is, will I be able to counsel effectively with others who come to me for advice. Will you help me? Will you stay in touch with me and write me and let me know about your victories—and even your defeats?"

The girls nodded and beamed. Yes, they would be eager to help in any way or form. We prayed together with our arms locked around each others' shoulders in a close circle. Christ was present, right in the middle of our circle.

Now I must sit down and answer the letter the two girls sent me. They are growing and sharing and learning—and so am I.

NOVEMBER/ *Monday Morning after Thanksgiving*

Every month is getting packed more tightly with new happenings, more learning, and deeper insights.

The children just left for the airport. We had a happy time together, except for some emotional struggles the girls are going through.

I never anticipated the new problems, but I should have! Since I was the one who always got attacked by my former church's gossip, I didn't think it could ever turn the other way. But it has.

Rollie is under attack now—and so is his future wife. Ever since they announced their wedding date, many tongues wag. I have no idea if anyone is talking to them, but some people make it their business to talk to my children. The boys can shrug it off. The two girls in college cannot. They go to a school of that denomination.

Kathy and Heidi have always been very sensitive toward people who tried to pump them for information about our family breakup. Kathy will mimic the "friends" for me. They come up and say, "Well, girls, and *how* is your mother?"

"Fine, thank you," the girls will assure the "friend," who then gives a searching glance, touches them on the sleeve, and lowers her voice.

"Now, how *is* she, really? You know what I mean."

Kathy says, "I look those people straight in their eyes and say, 'Ask her yourself, will you? I told you she is fine.' "

If people have the nerve to dig any farther, saying, "Well, I heard she is backslidden and not in the church anymore," or some such comment, those "friends" are asking for trouble. Kathy can really handle those questions!

The new gossip is different. When people come up and say, "I hear your father is courting," my girls don't know what to say. They didn't come to me about it, but they asked Elisabeth. She lives in our home now, since Cheri and Mary have found their own apartments. I didn't want Peter to be alone when I travel.

I overheard Kathy ask Elisabeth, "What is your biblical interpretation of divorce and remarriage? Do you think my dad will live in sin and adultery if he marries Diane?"

Elisabeth explained to all four of my children her interpretation of the issue and reassured them. "It's something your dad has to decide together with his fiancée before God," she said. "You can't make the decisions for them. Neither should you feel called to take any blame. Remember that Jesus loves us all and he wants to make *all* of us happy, if we let him."

The problem seemed settled until the girls came back from church yesterday morning. They had gone with a visiting friend to a church of his choice.

The pastor gave a sermon on divorce and remarriage. He made some very dogmatic statements. Kathy was in deep agony. Again, she didn't come to me, but went to Elisabeth for more help.

"I don't think a minister has *any* business to bring such an issue into his Sunday morning service," Elisabeth said rather spiritedly. "People come to church for comfort, strength, and fellowship. Since broken homes are so prevalent, many people come to a church for help. Such a service only deepens their sense of failure, condemns them further, and sends them home into deeper despair.

"The church may teach their doctrines, but the church service is not the time and place to bring it up." Elisabeth has strong convictions on this point!

"All right," Kathy said, still deeply troubled, "is there a Bible story somewhere that shows that Jesus even comforts or is kind to someone who has sinned, I mean a sin as big as adultery?"

"Yes," I heard Elisabeth say. "Remember the time that Jesus was in the Temple and the men brought a woman

to him? They had caught her in the act of adultery, and
they wanted Jesus to condemn her! Now there is no
doubt that she was guilty. There is not doubt that what
she did was wrong. But Jesus put the men on the
spot—the men, not the woman. He said that the one
who was without sin could throw the first stone at her.
The men all left. They had to admit that none of them
was sinless. Then Jesus turned to her and said, 'Where
are your accusers? Does no one accuse you?' 'No one,'
she answered. 'Neither do I condemn you. Go and sin no
more,' Jesus said to her. If anyone could have made that
woman suffer for her sins, Jesus could. But he didn't. He
was more interested in her than he was in making a point
about the sin of adultery. See, the men condemned her.
Jesus said, 'Neither do *I* condemn you!' It isn't our place
to condemn people. If Jesus forgives, how can we do less
than be kind and considerate—even when the person is
wrong?"

Thanks to a friend like Elisabeth, my girls went back to
college with new peace in their hearts.

When will we Christians ever learn that *love* is the fulfillment of God's law! I am more and more burdened, not
to defend interpretations of doctrines, but to let people
know that love and forgiveness are God's method of winning people into his kingdom.

I spoke at a big women's conference about this at the
beginning of my last tour. I watched hundreds of women
break into tears when I told them that I was praying for
the woman my former husband spends his time with. I
have been praying for her for a long time, ever since the
Lord told me one night, "Pray for the woman your husband is with."

I prayed for every woman whose name came back to
me through the children while he was dating around.
Now I am praying for a special blessing upon both of
them. It's not only for their sakes. It's for our children's
sakes, too. She also is a divorcee and has several chil-

dren. All those children will be affected by the happiness
or unhappiness of their parents. I have been pleading
with God to give my children's father a happy home. I
will continue to do so, for he needs it. I am praying that
the Holy Spirit will help them to have a forgiving spirit
toward their former mates, for their own and our children's sake. God can never give his full blessing on
something as long as we keep *any* grudge and unforgive-
ness in our hearts.

When I returned from my last seven-week tour just
before Thanksgiving, I found two letters in the pile of my
personal mail which touched me deeply. The two former
lesbian girls I correspond with wrote me separate letters.
Yvonne, the shy one, opened herself up and told me why
she became a homosexual in the first place. She wrote:

"About two weeks after I committed my life to my dear
Savior, the Lord showed me a consistent picture of my
life which I had never seen before. It has had a great
healing effect within me, and I would like to share his
wisdom about me with you.

"When I think back about what I wanted in a
friendship, I am aware of a blend of things that included
doing things together, talking with one another, and
helping one another grow, sharing dreams, making plans
and carrying them out, being committed and loyal to one
another, and sharing a deep, sweet love and affection for
one another. As a young child my memories of achieving
all that are pretty strong. Between my parents, my
brothers, and friends, I always found what I looked for.
My life seemed pretty full of such nourishing love. I remember myself as being a whole person in every way,
especially as one being open to receiving and retaining
the expressions of love. I've also had many occasions to
look back on my childhood and wish that I could be small
all over again, when I seemed to be such a perfect little
person.

"About the time that I was in grade six, it became dif-

ficult to find people who would be lasting friends. Somewhere along the way I had learned, more unconsciously
than consciously, that softness was not something I could
expect to express with boys. I went swimming in the river
with the boys and shared some degree of soft intimacy
again with a few girl friends. When it came to being soft
and intimate, there never seemed to be enough. I had
lots of love to give, but no one to give very much of it
to—as though what I had was 'too much.' My own desires for affectionate intimacy seemed to be sexual desire.
Whether this was the reason for my eventually having
sexual feelings for women or not, I don't really care. I
spent the next five years after my high school identifying
myself with the lesbian life-style, often becoming
hopelessly tangled in the emotional boil that is charac-
teristic of much of the gay community.

"I changed quite a bit during those five years. I really
believe that God's hand was on me when this woman
came into my life. It is because of her influence that I really began to soften up, and I'm sure that this greatly
aided my ability to respond to God and trust in his love
when it came time to accept Jesus, at the price of putting
my lesbian identity behind me. God did not even require
of me that I leave my lover, because she accepted Jesus,
too, and he has done the humanly impossible task of
changing our relationship into one that is all right in God's
sight. He loves us both so much.

"One of the beautiful insights I have received from this
perspective of my life was that I could see how, all along,
God made me just perfectly ready to receive his love. I
was looking to people in order to get it, but he always
intended me to receive it from him. Not only am I now
freed from that terrible scramble after something that is
never enough, but I can now free all my brothers and
sisters from that need to give me what *only* God can give
me. Hallelujah! It's going to take a while to become
whole this way, but his work has already come a long
way.

"I deeply feel that there are many, many people in the world whose dissatisfactions arise from 'never getting enough.' And yet they do not realize that it is God's love they are lacking. I feel that my story could echo the stories of thousands of people who are even happy, but could never find something to fill that place that is always crying for *more*!

"In my case, I tried to fill the void with a lesbian life-style. Other people fill it with overwork, or with their families, or with a belief that falls short of Jesus. Some people go against the traditions of our society, and some go with them. Some people look acceptable, and some do not.

"This brings me to another point of much concern. Homosexuality is given a very heavy hand by the churches that say anything about it at all. Where nothing is said, the atmosphere is one of condemnation for those who are or *ever have been* involved in it. Shelly wrote to you about this. . . ."

This is what Shelly said about that point in her letter:

"Because of our past we are extremely sensitive to the attitude of condemnation toward homosexuals. We are struggling with a sometimes subtle, sometimes blatant attitude of prejudice concerning this particular area of sin within the church. Your sincere, loving attitude toward us has helped to alleviate our many fears and meet our new needs as young Christians. There are serious obstacles of condemnation directed at homosexuals from a large population of believers in Jesus. In you we found at least one Christian who had a perspective on the problem that was realistic and acceptable to Yvonne and myself.

"I am greatly concerned that a self-righteous attitude of many believers will continue to keep homosexuals in bondage and prevent them from possibly gathering enough courage to walk through the doors of God's churches to hear his word in a noncondemning environment.

"There *is* a church in the U.S.A. and Canada where

homosexuals are welcome to worship God in an atmosphere of noncondemnation. Perhaps you have heard of this church? The noncondemning atmosphere is needed; however, both Yvonne and I were grieved to read the following words in a newsletter, published by one of those churches:

" 'The ——————— Community Church is part of a fellowship which came into being out of need of many persons to worship God and seek spiritual goals in a setting which does not condemn, object, or ignore them for that which they know to be part of their basic need.

" *'All* people regardless of their demoninational affiliation are invited to join with us in affirming that "there is therefore now *no* condemnation to them which are in Christ Jesus" (Romans 8:1).' "

Shelly continued in her letter: "I am copying this excerpt from their newsletter as it was printed. The word which was obviously supposed to be denominational, is printed by mistake 'demoninational.' Upon reading the basis for noncondemnation in this church, Yvonne and I were aghast that God's Holy Word would be so misrepresented. The verse these people quote is incomplete. They seem to neglect the *whole* truth! 'There is therefore now no condemnation to them which are in Christ Jesus, *who walk not after the flesh, but after the Spirit*' (Romans 8:1).

"It seems to us that many people are going to be deceived by this false doctrine, who otherwise might come to accept and know the full truth of Jesus Christ. If only our traditional churches would demonstrate the love God expects of his children! If they would only *love* those many, many people in our society who are in the bondage of the enemy and do not *know* that they can be *free* and have peace in our Lord Jesus."

Here I sit crying again! After all the laughter and happiness that we had in our home while we were all together, while giving thanks and praise to God for the abundance and blessings we can have in this great land of ours, I still sit and cry. Am I ungrateful? Do I feel sorry for myself?

God knows my heart. He knows why and for whom I cry!

I cry for my girls who wonder if they have a right to defend their father. I cry for Yvonne who felt she had to become a lesbian to find enough love. I ache for Shelly who pleads for acceptance. I suffer with Ellen who carries scars on her body and soul.

Oh, Lord, is there no healing for all the heartaches and confusion?

There is! Love covers a multitude of sin. Love heals and permits a new beginning. Love never faileth! God must teach all of us *his* kind of love!

DECEMBER/ *Friday Night*

I never thought that four fast weeks could influence and mature a life as much as this last month has molded me.

Little did I dream what all God had in store for me in such a short time. Of course, the Lord always plants special seeds ahead of time. The new learnings grow slowly at first, unobserved and often not recognized at all. And all of a sudden they burst into bloom! Much has bloomed for me this month!

The first sign that God had something special for me came at that special women's retreat, where I told the ladies about my divorce and God's teachings of love. Their theme was *Set Free,* and the whole place was decorated with orange painted butterflies who had come out of their cocoons. They had been set free to fly! What a symbol!

While I gave the opening address a live butterfly flew in through the open door, circled all around me, and finally lit behind me on my empty speaker's chair. A ripple went through the audience. I stopped my speaking for a moment and someone told me what had just happened.

God said, "It's my love message for you. You are out of the cocoon, you are *free*. You can fly again!"

I was overwhelmed by it, but really didn't know what God meant. I finished the meeting and wondered. That night I asked, "Why do you say, I now can *fly* again, Lord? I thought I was free!"

"Trust me," God said. "Wait and see. I have much happiness and joy and contentment for your future. I also have some new messages to give through you."

I didn't have much time to speculate over what was coming. I was too busy with my work at hand.

After I had shared with more than a thousand women, giving my second message on what God had done for me—a divorced woman, who needed to be set free—the floodgates of tears and love opened. It was the first time that I spoke to a large audience about my divorce.

I watched a miracle take place. I had challenged that conservative group to take the black sheep and the singles and the divorced and the repentant sinners into their midst and love them freely. I had used my favorite phrase again, "The Evangelicals are the only group who shoot their wounded!" I also had quoted a sentence one woman had said to me months before: "The most lonely place for a divorced person to be is in the church."

I could have added that widows and people who've never married can feel just as lonely.

I long ago came to the conclusion that the American society is so sex-oriented that even the Christians are strongly influenced and biased by it. It colors the Christian fellowship even in areas that have outwardly nothing to do with the Hollywood symbols of sex and its appeal. Couples seldom include the single person. They either feel odd or threatened by the extra person. The wives and husbands worry that the single person will "steal" their mates. Or they feel there is something "wrong" with them, or they would be married.

If singles get together, they are often subject to suspi-
cion, gossip, or judging. After all, what are they up to?
Are they spending time together to make out? Friendships
of the same sex are under worse scrutiny. Just in case
someone could have something "wrong" in his personality, better keep a safe distance away!

Jesus did not practice such a "righteous distance." He
could have stayed away from singles and outcasts. He
was truly sinless, blameless, and pure. But he didn't! He
came and gave his all: his life, his reputation when he ate
with sinners, his former position in heaven, his unconditional love and forgiveness—he came to set us all *free!*

The women were stunned by what I had to say, but
they let the Holy Spirit do the work he longed to do. He
began to set people free: of hate, of self-pity, of self-
righteousness. I not only stood after the meeting for two
hours, holding woman after woman who wept on my
shoulder (often because I had told her story when I told
mine), but I listened to "normal" women confess their
judgmental attitudes and harshness toward their suffering
sisters.

I was showered by so much Christian love and acceptance that I felt like a new woman. "Is that what you
meant by the message of the butterfly?" I asked the Lord.

"Wait and see," God said to me. "Trust me, I have
great happiness and joy and contentment for you."

I did have much happiness on my tour. I spoke in several prisons and watched God's love set men free. In one
institution twenty-three young people gave their hearts to
Christ. Our office began to be flooded with mail. It still is
flooded!

After four weeks in the midwestern states I flew for
three weeks to Europe to speak to the armed forces of
the U.S.A. in Germany, Holland, and England. What a
privilege, what a joy I had! How lonely our troops are
over there, especially around the holidays. I spoke and
smiled and told them what a special spot they all had in
my heart. I thanked them for being in Europe.

"The Europeans are forgetting why you are in Europe," I said to the women and men who were able to attend the rallies and chapel services I spoke for. "Please, don't ever forget that you are here to preserve freedom. And as Christians you are God's means to heal the land."

Those men do need healing everywhere; the problems are overwhelming. Alcohol and drugs are often the only way out for lonely soldiers and their families. Suicide is more frequent over the Christmas season. Why must people be so desperate and forsaken, in prisons, in the army, in lonely apartments, in bars, when we Christians have the answer for them? I have a deep compassion for lonely people now. I know how they feel!

Sometimes I have an overpowering need to be held, to be told that I am loved, that I am "normal," that I don't have to walk alone for the rest of my life. I probably will have such desperate moments every so often, but I know now that I can handle them. I am not afraid of being alone anymore.

I *chose* to be alone this month. In these last four short weeks I was set truly free by my own choice and will.

I know now what God meant when he said that I could fly again, that I *was* out of my cocoon. God gave me a choice. I could get married again and give up the stigma of being a divorced woman, or go on with him alone. The choice was mine, and I could have married without feeling guilty toward God or men.

I don't know if I will ever be able to talk about the special gift of love I received this last month! I knew I was loved and I loved this man. I know now beyond the shadow of a doubt that I am a normal, warm-blooded woman who could make a fine and deeply respected husband happy. I didn't let him come to the point of a marriage proposal. I didn't want him to feel rejected. We kept our relationship above gossip and reproach. We are friends. I have always believed that the highest form of love is friendship. I believe it more than ever!

I had a choice and I made it. For his sake and mine, we shall stay friends alone.

Peter asked me if I was planning to get married. He likes the man. I told my son that I would if I were just a normal Christian woman. But I am not; I have been called to serve God in a special way. If we got married, it would destroy my ministry. People wouldn't forgive me. We are both divorced. They would shoot both of us all over again. I thought it through long and carefully before I decided.

I know we could make it. My present ministry would be destroyed, but we could serve God in other ways. We both love Jesus with all our hearts. We pray together. We have wept together over our situation. He would provide male companionship for Peter. It would protect my close friendship with Elisabeth. Her soul and mine are knit together like David's and Jonathan's of the Old Testament. If I stay alone, we probably will be gossiped about. It happened with Mary, it will happen with her—or him. Whoever will be my close friend will come under attack.

It would be so much easier to get married and face life together, even under such circumstances. I know that Jesus wouldn't condemn us, he would bless us.

Tonight I stood alone on top of a mountain. I watched the stars come out one by one. Jesus and I talked. I thanked him. "Jesus," I said, "thank you for setting me free. As long as I *had* to be alone, I served you because I had nowhere else to go. When you gave me the chance for a new life here on earth, a man's deep love and a happy married home, you gave me a beautiful choice. I want to thank you for it. Jesus, you know my decision: I need nobody but you. You are sufficient. You are my Lord and Master, my Husband, my Lover, my Provider, my closest Friend. Lord, I *want* to serve. When I spoke to the women at the retreat, I ended my message by saying that I knew I was a crushed leaf. I wanted to be the kind we used in my childhood to lay on wounds for healing.

At that time I didn't know that you would give me a
choice of becoming a whole leaf again, someone who
would again be accepted as 'normal' in our society. I'd
rather stay crushed, Lord. I'd rather stay with you alone,
and I thank you for it.

"Bless all those I love, my Jesus. If a heart is lonely because of my decision, please, make it up to him. Be everything to him, as you are to me. I love you, Jesus. I
love you more than anybody or anything."

I sat under the stars and remembered a moment in
Europe, just a few short weeks ago. I had spoken in an
American high school on one of the bases, and the young
people had received me with much enthusiasm.

A young black teacher ate lunch with me after the
meeting. He was a turned-on Christian of the Catholic
faith and a very outgoing person. "I don't know what you
have," he said to me. "I can say what you say and nobody listens. You tell it to the kids, and they stand up and
whistle and clap. I feel often like I am beating my head
against the wall. It all looks so hopeless. I often wonder
why I am wasting my time over here. We have so many
problems, like drugs, alcohol, mixed-up students from
broken homes . . ."

I looked at him and smiled. I knew how he felt. I had
felt like that very often in my life. "Friend," I said, and it
was God who gave me the words, "you are still at the
age when you believe that you can change the world. I
have gone past that age. I am too old for that. All I want
to do is to light some candles in the darkness. We cannot
get rid of the darkness, but even if we light one solitary
candle, the darkness can never overcome that little light!"

The teacher's eyes lit up and he said, "I shall never
forget what you said. I will remember it when I get discouraged. I shall always remember it!"

I will, too.

I drove by myself down the mountains in the darkness.
I wasn't alone. Jesus was so close that I could feel his

arms around me. I shall never be alone again—and I shall light candles for searching hearts. It is more than enough for me. It is happiness, joy, and contentment—and it is all in him alone!